WHO STOLE my Soul?

A DIALOGUE WITH THE DEVIL ON THE MEANING OF LIFE

Vishwa Prakash

Synergy Books

We appreciate your comments.
Email us at **feedback@whostolemysoul.com**

Who Stole My Soul?: A Dialogue with the Devil on the Meaning of Life
Published by Synergy Books
PO Box 80107
Austin, TX 78758

For more information about our books, please write to us, call 512.478.2028, or visit our website at www.synergybooks.net.

Publisher's Cataloging in Publication available upon request.

LCCN: 2009925810

ISBN 13: 978-0-9823140-5-0
ISBN 10: 0-9823140-5-1

This book does not dispense medical advice or prescribe in any way the use of any technique or form of treatment for any physical, medical or mental problems, either directly or indirectly. The knowledge offered in this book is of a general nature for educational purposes to help readers in their quest for emotional and spiritual well being. The author, publisher and printer do not guarantee the accuracy or actual workability of the messages and final recommendations contained in this book, and assume no responsibility for the impressions, actions and outcomes of the reader.

10 9 8 7 6 5 4 3 2 1

To

My mother

Vimla,

who is

an ocean of love

and my inspiration

for this book

"I sought my soul,
my soul I could not see

I sought my God,
my God eluded me

I sought my brother,
I found all three"

—Baba Amte

(who led the light to the loneliest, the lost, the least and the last)

CONTENTS

PROLOGUE

Suppose, just suppose, that your soul had deserted your body. Whatever your *soul* is, whatever you deem it to be. Would that leave you richer or poorer, bigger or smaller, with more or with less? Would you be dead or alive?

The spiritual supremos say that your soul is not part of your body, just dwells there. If that is so, then some years ago, mine was stolen and I was left with the hull, just the shell of my body. I continued a half-life filled with fear of what had become of me. I could eat and drink, but not be merry anymore. Because my soul was missing.

Where did it go? What was it up to? Who stole my soul?

If God is the guardian of souls, then surely it is the devil who dislodges and drives them away. The grim reaper. Another name for the Devil, or Satan, the anti-God.

I wanted to ask the devil, "What did you do? Why and how did you seduce my soul away from me?" I looked into the dark recesses of my imagination, into the world of my fears and fancies. For isn't that where the devil lurks?

In the netherworld of my dreams, I *felt* the presence of the devil even as I feared him. And so, I beseeched this strange force to show himself to me and to respond to my fears. The fears that flooded my being in flashes and sapped my strength.

And the devil was forthcoming.

One day, in a reverie, an overpowering aura entered my field of perception. I lay in wonderment, mesmerized by this unseen energy. I rubbed my eyes, but there was nothing to see, nothing to touch, nothing to hear.

The Presence seemed to reassure me that there was nothing to say. Some telepathic messages raced into my brain, my heart, my very being. I felt plugged in to, conjoined to a greater force. My apprehension was momentary, for through a kind of cosmic connection, my unease was stilled. One little blip of a thought, transmitted in a nanosecond, carried and conveyed volumes of content to respond to the queries of my heart.

Not a word exchanged. Nor even a glance. I seemed to have a direct psychic line to the Presence. Before I could ask, "Are you the devil?" I had my answer: "I am whom you seek."

And so, in a dream state of heightened awareness, in crystal clarity, began my exchanges with Satan, the demon, the devil—call him what you wish.

This book is an account of the psychic conversation I had with the anti-God. It is an outpouring of my troubled heart. Of my fears and fantasies that have continued to haunt and darken my life.

It is first a search for my soul, which went missing, enamored by a new lover, and then a reconciliation with it. The captivation of my soul exposed me to a new scenery of life, the promise of which will likewise lure your own soul. This book will sweep your soul away, then bring it back through its pages, rejuvenated and refreshed. If you see your own reflection mirrored back through its chapters, then it is no coincidence. It was meant to be. Everything happens for a reason, and today this book has come to your hand for a reason.

❧❦❧

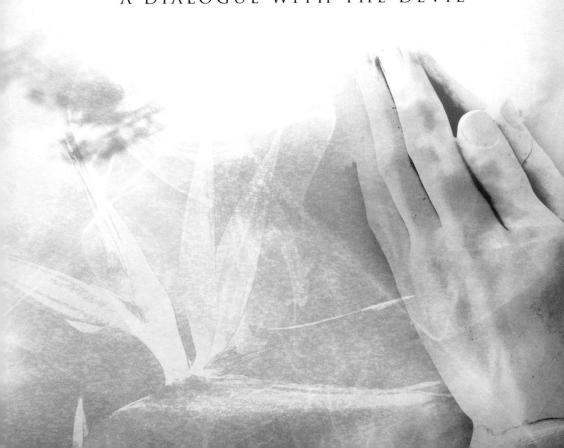

A DIALOGUE WITH THE DEVIL

CHAPTER 1

DIALOGUE

BETWEEN

THE DEVIL

Angel of darkness, antichrist, archfiend, demon, king of hell, monster,
the profoundly evil adversary of God and humanity,
the devil and chief evil spirit.

AND

VISHWA

Confused and directionless in a world where good things seem to happen to
bad people, and bad things to good people.

Hark! Who dares to disturb me when I'm resting?

 Just me, sir. I'm sorry to bother you, but I wanted a few words with you, and I thought you could help me.

 Help?! The only help I can give you is to gobble you up before your time. Get lost before I turn you into ash.

 I'm sure you can do that, Mr. D—it's just that I believe you're the best person to counsel me. You specialize in causing disharmony and disorder, so surely you'll understand my dilemmas and doubts—my internal turmoil.

 Don't irritate me; I can end your life this minute. I'm the anti-God—all that puts fear and suffering into you weepy, wimpy humans. You can believe what you want, but I'm sure my views run counter to yours.

 Precisely why I need you, sir! I need an opposing view because I'm full of doubts.

I'd like to understand why the world is so unfair from the one who makes it so, and that's you! I'm confused about conflicting feelings in my heart: loving and helping at one moment, angry and grasping the next. I have so many fears, doubts, and internal turmoil, and I'm sure you can help me.

 Hmm. Turmoil is what I thrive on. Tell me, do you often feel angry?

 I feel easily irritated, sometimes to the extreme. I get annoyed about why people behave the way they do. Sometimes, in my moments of frustration and chagrin, I've secretly wished horrible things for so many people. My entire system goes out of whack when somebody's ridden roughshod over my feelings. I'm riveted to the bitterness and resentment and can't think straight.

 What dark thoughts do you have?

In the secret world of my imagination, I have been a murderer many times over. I have been the policeman of people's actions, their jury and judge and finally their executioner too.

I have met hundreds of smooth-talking tricksters. I often wished them dead—not just dead, but horribly dead. And I am impatient and intolerant of the slightest ignorance or arrogance or bad manners. My inner monster spares nobody, not my neighbor, not my colleagues, not my friends, not my relatives.

In my dreams, I have ravished many a woman, and why? Because she looked ravishing.

The loud, animated sales pitch, the grouch who can't wait his turn, the man who honks in a traffic jam. I've wished a giant hammer would squish them all into a pancake. So you see, if it's my Godlessness that's under the microscope, who better than the anti-God to guide me?

> *"What other dungeon is so dark as one's own heart! What jailer so inexorable as one's self."*
> —Nathaniel Hawthorne

Hmm. I see potential in you. Maybe one day you can graduate to real-world crimes. You might even make a good assistant for my work.

I feel as if I'm a fake and a fraud to put up a smiling and nonchalant face to the world while brooding on black images.

Aha! So you think crooked thoughts?

Yes. I think and feel spiteful thoughts, to hit back, even viciously. In my despair and agony, I can think of nothing but revenge. I visualize the worst punishment for the person who's caused my misery. The guilt of my hidden crimes is a living hell, and I have nowhere to bury it. In the outer world, one can pay the penalty and lighten one's burden. Society forgives but may not forget. But in my secret world there is nobody to forgive my crimes—it is up to me to forget them. Any regret and remorse is never totally purged, and the venom stays.

> *"Everyone is a moon, and has a dark side which he never shows to anybody."*
> —Mark Twain

Why don't you just vent out the venom?

The legal and moral systems of the world don't permit force. Things don't always happen as they could or should. The crooked seem to thrive just as successfully as the righteous. Why do bad things happen to good people, and good things happen to bad people? Why do all the stupid, stuck-up people in the world get all the good luck? I try very hard to be loving and honest and good, but this isn't what brings social and financial success in life. Why is that so? Are we all frustrated?

Welcome to the club of around seven billion of you on the planet!

I don't know if it's normal to be so suspicious, but this is what I've become in order to survive and succeed: wary and watchful all the time. I see some covert cause in anything that doesn't fit into the rat-race formula of human actions. To me, a sugary-sweet smile obviously has some selfish motive behind it.

So it does, and so it should. You've read the human condition perfectly. It's all about "me first." You're very much a part of the animal kingdom where everyone is a predator.

I thought humans were different. We have a brain, a heart, and a soul. Don't you think we're higher than the laws of the jungle? Animals don't have guilt.

Did you hear me? If you want to pussyfoot around, then get lost! But if it's force you want to learn, then I'm the one for you.

Life's not that easy. Almost every bit of learning and advice is to be overcareful, fend, foster, and fight. You're told to fear whatever dangers may be lurking around and taught that aggressive pursuit of your ends is the only way up.

Yup. That's good advice. Grab what you can. Go for it and watch out for others who'll grab what's yours.

Oh, I can be as lean and mean as the success mantra teaches. And when people get in the way, I get irritated and exasperated. The smallest of everyday annoyances can turn me from a docile dove to an angry tiger. I wish I could teach them all a lesson.

Aha! The medieval schoolmaster with the whip. Don't you all picture yourselves this way—the know-it-all savior of the world? What's new? It's your primitive urge to preach and to punish. That's the way it is. It's a jungle out there, and you have to fight for your place in it. Your teeth and claws should always stay sharp. Can't you handle your feelings?

That's not easy. With so many unfair and unreasonable things happening, I've become suspicious, scornful, and skeptical of everything and everybody.

Growing up is a process of rejection and dejection. Your ardor emerges battered and bruised. Better get used to it.

So skepticism is our lot?

To a large extent.

I might have carried it too far. I sneer at the slightest sign of zeal I see in people. Instinctively, I suspect the worst in every human action, an ulterior motive. I fear that being so suspicious has killed off my verve and vibrancy.

Ah, fear! Do you feel it often?

I'm constantly in a state of worry and fear. The fear of horrible things that could happen to both myself and my loved ones. Fear driven by the guilt of how venomous my feelings and thoughts can be. Then the fear that I may lose all that I've worked so hard to achieve. I'm constantly haunted by one fear or another.

Fear is what I strike everybody with. It is a great disciplinary tool.

I seem obsessed by fear and worry. I suppose it's because throughout our lives, we're threatened by the dire consequences of failure. We're taught to think of the worst, plan for the "what if." The fear that's put into us as a prodding mechanism perhaps makes us too wary of situations, people, our own feelings and motives. Isn't that so?

Are you talking about yourself or the world at large?

Both. I think all of us have lots of fears.

Fear is my best friend. I thrive on heaping it on you humans.

I've become automatically fearful and judgmental of people and their motives. And that's why I'm here, talking to you. About my fears and doubts.

You're no different than anybody else, and the fears and doubts are here to stay. So what's new? When and how are you troubled by your fears and fantasies?

Some of my fantasies are fleeting, and some are long and lingering. They visit me as movie clips, vivid and as often as a million a minute. The visions are never there by invitation but creep in by stealth. I am not their willing host but a slave to their whims as they overpower me in broad daylight, hijacking my senses.

Most of my illusions float by even as I'm at work or in the shower or on the bus. Anytime, anywhere. Sometimes they surface as a deep emotion and take over all of my body systems. I am now in a panic, now in a blind rage, and now in chagrin at my own impotence to fend off the attack on my sensibilities.

> *"Each of us is something of a schizophrenic personality, tragically divided against ourselves."*
> —Martin Luther King, Jr

That's the right way for your fears to hit you. Without a warning. But come on, surely you didn't entreat me to come here just to air this banal blah-blah? What's the specific reason you sought me out?

Oh, I have a strong reason, Mr. D. Do please hear me out.

Go ahead, have your say, but stay to the point!

Until recently, I could handle my intolerance, anger, skepticism, and fear. I didn't think much of it. But then, a strange force drew the soul out of me, separated me from my soul. And this threw me off balance.

You mean you died? This is bizarre!

In a way, I both died and became reborn. My soul wasn't physically parted from my body, but emotionally. It developed a mind of its own, disconnected from the leanings of my brain. Before my soul deserted me, it would join me in whatever I did and went along with whatever pleasures I undertook. But once it was stolen away from me, it went its own way with whatever it liked, whatever tickled its fancy.

Ah, now I understand.

Before my soul ran away with this mysterious and magnetic force, I was okay with my life. I could eat, drink, and be merry with ease, and my soul didn't bother me with any pangs or pain. I was free to drink in all the goodies of the world without any twinge of self-doubt or impropriety about my worldly behavior.

What worldly behavior?

My hard-as-nails attitude to the world. My never-say-die stance toward achievement. My scoffing at the soppy sentimentalism of others. My aggressive approach, bordering on the arrogant.

That's the approach I like. Shoot-to-kill.

Oh sure, the annoyances were part of life, but I wasn't bothered as such by any guilt or recriminations for my thoughts and actions. I jealously protected my growing turf with pride, and the go-get mantra worked wonders. If anybody ventured to belittle or block my ascent in life, then I was quick to put down any such designs on my poise. I was conscious of my role in the social hierarchy and comfortable with my acquisitive character.

What happened to part you from your idyllic life?

My soul was stolen away from me, seduced by a strange force. And that left me a body with a missing soul. That is when my world fell apart.

I'm puzzled. Speak clearly.

My soul was romancing something that caught its fancy and was absorbed in this amusement. I wasn't physically separated from it, but emotionally parted. Left alone, I began to lose my zest for all the good things I had so painstakingly amassed in my life. The pride from my achievements began to lose its shine and seemed diffused and distant. My assertiveness, which I prized as my greatest strength, now seemed to become limp and humble. And I began to have disconnected flashes.

What's that?

I would be standing at a party, cocktail in hand, and for some reason the sound seemed switched off. I could see hands flailing, lips moving animatedly, but could hear no sound. My favorite action hero in the movies now appeared as a comical and absurd stuntman. The new contract, the new deal in my work had brought in a windfall but could only draw a yawn from me. The calamity of losing out on a big investment drew another yawn. My world seemed to have fallen flat, the fizz gone.

You became withdrawn?

I seemed to have lost interest in the raucous tales of my buddies and was drawn more toward quieter, composed company. My palate seemed to have become disconnected with my taste buds. I lost my zest for many of the things I'd relished before.

You missed your soul?

You could say so. I witnessed the joy of my soul in its newfound romance. At first I vicariously rejoiced in this, but then my heart was increasingly drawn to the new luster of my soul. It was so immersed in its joy.

Who, or what, is it that stole your soul from you?

I thought it was a passing fancy, like a flirtation, but over time it became evident that the fantasy was real. Increasingly, my soul preferred to stay with its newfound love and left me high and dry.

I repeat, who or what is it that stole your soul away?

An interest, a leaning. Something that held sway over it, appealed to it, and swept it off its feet.

I can't wait forever! What?

It was an activity of charitable giving—a cause meant for individual and social good. This enchanted and entranced my soul so much that it refused to return to its home in my heart. It became riveted on its newfound joy and excused itself from joining me in my lifestyle.

Don't talk in riddles. Explain yourself clearly.

For some reason, this charitable activity brought a glow to my soul's face. A spring to its step, a new excitement in the way it held itself. And that's the *who* and *what* that stole my soul.

So a charitable work enchanted your soul? That's silly!

That's how I felt in the beginning, but as the months passed, the silliness became serious. My soul visited my heart from time to time, but in an absent manner, with a faraway look, not really interested in joining me in my everyday life.

You mean your hard-nosed lifestyle?

Yes. And since my soul was missing, I began to see my values and lifestyle as hollow and superficial. I proceeded to question the combative code I had lived by and my grasping attitude to life. Whatever had earlier motivated me seemed to hold less meaning now.

And this threw me off balance. I felt like a fish out of water.

So what did you do?

I followed my soul. We had a few disagreements, more like lovers' spats. But my soul is my soul. It led me by the nose, and I had no choice but to follow it.

I was forced to rearrange my lifestyle and my priorities to accommodate the wishes of my soul. The understanding was clear: my soul was to be the steering wheel and I the engine of this car.

With some suspicion and skepticism, I tagged along with my soul in its charitable giving, a kind of healing movement. I began spending increasing amounts of my time and money on this cause. And that is when I became befuddled and beaten by what came over me. What started out as an act of humoring my soul bulldozed my sensibilities. Often I felt foolish putting important and pressing matters on the back burner to accommodate the demands of this seemingly frivolous fad. I feared being ridiculed by my friends and relatives, who sometimes scoffed at me. Yet I felt a strange satisfaction, a gush of warmth in my heart like I've never felt before.

I can see that you go where the skirt goes. You gave in to your soul.

I had no choice. I now sense a sort of inner glow when I offer my giving. It casts a joyful and soothing spell on me that just refuses to go away. I feel profoundly peaceful.

Ha! That's your gullibility, your impressionable childishness. You're just bowled over by a passing fancy. I pity you for being the Simple Simon that you are!

You could be right. I was taught to be rational and realistic. Not to be swayed by wacky whims. My innate skepticism is challenging my own behavior. I have questions that need answers, and I'm afraid some of my questions may need questioning too!

How interesting. Girl walks off, boy begs and pleads, girl returns on her terms, subdues boy, boy and girl live forever in domestic harmony and bliss. I've seen better paperbacks.

That's a snide and cynical way to put it. I sometimes can't believe what I've become and why. I confided in you about how crafty and cunning I can be. I can be devious and deceitful when I want to, and I've already described my intolerance and underlying aggression to you.

And now I find myself in a situation that's confusing. I've stumbled on entirely new feelings that I can't reconcile with my cold and calculating self. The feelings from joining my soul in giving and healing have overpowered me and my way of life. My confusion is that this is not consistent, not in sync with the time-tested hunt and hoard mantra that's worked for me before.

Which brings me to you. If I'm questioning my suspicious, mistrustful side, then I figured I should share these thoughts with the master of mistrust to sort myself out.

Hmm…It's always nice to meet new admirers. What's your background?

I'm just a small-time nobody, bewildered with the new twists in my life.

I mean, what you do, what's your line of work?

Oh, I'm self-employed. I run a small textile design firm. I've had my fair share of success and good fortune in life.

Aha! You have a guilt complex. Or maybe you felt the do-gooder sensation. A common folly.

I feel cloaked in a kind of calm when I'm occupied with this charitable giving. I can't explain why.

Yawn. So you want to share some bleeding-heart story?

I'm mesmerized by the soothing influence of the charitable work that's enchanted my soul. Yet I'm perplexed, and I wonder whether my feelings make any sense. So I really need to talk it over, especially in the light of my rugged and ruthless rise to success.

Conventional wisdom tells us to maximize our gains and focus our energies to further our material ends. I'm bewildered that I'm actually enjoying doing the opposite of my training. One side of me tells me to fight, grab, and keep. The other side is actually enjoying doing the bang opposite, which is to back off, give, and let go. I'm at a loss.

> *"One who doesn't suffer from inner conflict is a lunatic."*
>
> —Jawaharlal Nehru,
> Indian Prime Minister

Just your sickly sentimentalism. It's a personality flaw, a passing phase. Join me in one of my daily destruction drives and I'll cure you.

Do please hear me out. I'm baffled by my bizarre behavior. I want to put my experiences through a sanity test. You're the devil, so you won't be swayed by any sweet talk of charity, goodness, and love. You'll shoot down any flimsy findings I may have. That's why I sought *you* rather than anybody else.

Looks like some high-hat, smooth-tongued goody-goody's been talking to you. I can fix that easily!

I don't need any fixing. I need you to be the face of my questioning, non-believing self. I need a sounding board, an examination of ideas that question my own. Who better for this cross-questioning of my dark side than the Lord of Darkness?

Look, normally I don't have time for all this bumble-babble. But I'm flattered that one of you dumb mortals wants a heart-to-heart with me. So let's talk, but on one condition. If you begin to bore me with some bombastic Godly spiel, then I'll just lick my lips and chomp your head off.

> *"God and the devil are fighting for mastery, and the battlefield is the heart of man."*
>
> —Dostoyevsky

Come on, Mr. D—all I need from you is your viewpoint on my dilemma and doubts. I feel unbridled joy when I'm in my charitable mode. A great lightness of being, almost rapturous. But beneath my exterior lie mountains of anger and guilt. And fear. And mistrust. So I wonder whether I'm a fake, a two-faced trickster leading a duplicitous life, living a lie.

Each of you on earth is devious and double-dealing. What's new?

The contradiction this presents. I'm impatient and intolerant one moment, caring and giving the next. How do I reconcile my scornful, supercilious side with my sympathetic self?

Ah. Self-doubt, planted there by me, the anti-God, the inner voice that can scoff and laugh at your own self. I rather like you, and might just spare you out of curiosity to see where your monkeying around will take you! What are your doubts?

About the act of giving, about the meaning of life, and what really makes us tick. I need to talk about the right and wrong, good and bad of this, to understand myself better. Am I good, or am I evil? What's the logic?

Evil has no logic to answer to. That's me—the force that enters your hearts at will, pumping in feelings of grapple, grab, and get. Fear and guilt are my trusted tools. You've dared to sneak into my domain and disturb my peace. But you've also piqued my interest.

Oh, thanks, Mr. D. So you agree?

Look, I'm Satan, and by my very nature must oppose any charity and goodness. So you're wasting your time.

To validate myself, I need my negative feelings to stand up to rigid, one-sided negative questioning, and for this there's none better than the lord of negativity to help me.

I can mirror your doubts, but what I do is perforce against the human grain. So let me understand once again: All that you want is for me to question and test your beliefs.

That's right.

That's a strange request, confining me to narrow, negative questioning. I'm curious about where this conversation will lead to, but just keep your emotional babbling and blubbering in check. *One* hint of any self-righteous zealotry from you, and I'll seal your fate.

It's a deal. And thanks in advance, Mr. D.

CHAPTER 2

WHO STOLE MY SOUL?

 So, who and what exactly stole your soul?

 The charitable activity it's drawn to. It seduced my soul, stole it from me.

 Be specific. What's the charity that so charmed and captivated your soul?

 It's not a conventional charity. It's more offbeat. And now that I've reclaimed my soul, I could say it's charmed and captivated all of me, soul included.

 So you now speak as one?

 I've already clarified that my separation from my soul was never physical but one of emotional leaning—a matter of taste and moral inclination. My soul pushed me toward certain actions, and when it found a certain elation and rapture in this novel undertaking, it cajoled me not only to stay with it but to make it a growing part of my life.

 Stop beating around the bush! Just get on with it. What's bowled you over? Wowed you, as you say?

Many years ago, I read about a laugh doctor in India who makes people laugh in public parks. I don't know why or how the soul inside me was drawn to what he did, but it convinced me to fly over, meet with him, and even train under him.

You did what?!

I learned how to make people laugh.

Are you insane? Don't you have something better to do?

Please, sir. I'm not mad. I learned the technique on a whim of my soul, but over time I felt strange sensations that challenged the conventional wisdom. That's a part of me that I still need to resolve, but in the meantime I took this step with my soul as the guide.

This is laughable!

That's okay. I'm used to people laughing at me. Well, laughing *with* me is more accurate.

The only laughing I do is when I'm closing in for the kill, or when I'm snuffing out hopes and aspirations.

My kind of laughter isn't some sort of battle cry like yours. It's more human, comes from the heart and creates cheer and joy. It brings people closer together, and they share their joys and sorrows. It drives away depression and dejection.

I had a premonition that something fishy was coming out of you. But this is preposterous! Cheer and joy are against my grain, and I'll have nothing to do with you!

Please, Mr. D, do hear me out!

This is crazy. In my time I've seen many a daft person, but this is bizarre!

As a matter of fact, I felt the same way. I was born shy and tongue-tied and really looked up to people who had the right words, the confidence and wit, and made people laugh. So when my inner self came across this laughing guru in India, I thought "why not?" Turns out that this is the biggest decision I made in my life.

A big decision to become the biggest fool. You're batty.

That may be true, but I'm beyond caring. My curiosity was piqued at how this laugh doctor was making thousands laugh, and opening up new laughter clubs around the world. So I went on to train under Dr. Kataria in India and learned *laughteryoga*—the technique.

You needed training to laugh?

No. I needed training on how to make others laugh.

That requires training?

Yes. I'm just your average dimwitted nobody. I often get the joke too late, or not at all. I think of the right things to say long after the moment's gone. So I thought it would be a good idea to learn the ways and means of making people laugh.

What do you do? Clown around? Mimicry? Jokes? Do you get drunk or just be your natural buffoonish self?

Well, actually, your last description comes close. In a way, each child is a natural buffoon who laughs just for the heck of it. But when we grow up, we all somehow turn self-conscious and become grim and gruff.

Within each of us there's a child whose enthusiasm was bulldozed with prohibitions on the natural effervescence of childhood. Our natural chattering and chirping was corrected by our elders and channeled into socially acceptable mannerisms. As children, we laughed hundreds of times a day, without jokes and humor, but as we grow up we laugh less and less.

So you clown around? You must be kidding.

You're right! I *am* kid-ing. I take adults back to their kid selves, to their inhibition-free, carefree laughter. Kids are naturally enthusiastic, amused, and amazed with everything and can laugh

> "In every real man a child is hidden that wants to play."
> —Friedrich Nietzsche

spontaneously. So yes, the technique of making people laugh is to let loose the kid within them. It's called *laughteryoga*. By adding play to yogic breathing exercises, we touch your heart with initially a kind of induced laughter. This soon becomes free-flowing and contagious.

You mean this is fake laughter to start with? A sham?

I agree that we begin our laughter routine as a put-on, self-induced action—but laughter is laughter, and it turns into the real thing very quickly. And when you laugh, your worries blank out; you reach your heart and lose yourself in ripples of belly laughter.

That's not even funny; it's farcical! With the stresses and strains of twenty-first-century life, who has the time and inclination to clown around like you?

Oh! It's precisely because the twenty-first century has so many stresses and strains that people need to clown around. Laughter's a guaranteed way to de-stress, de-strain, and decompress. People make time for whatever they enjoy.

This childish game, this tittering around, can't possibly interest too many of you.

No, sir! Today there are some ten thousand laughter clubs in sixty countries. Our laughter has really caught on like a wildfire, and it's now a large and respected international movement. Just as people go to the gym for physical exercise, they attend laughteryoga sessions for a good bout of laughter, which is a great exercise of the mind and body.

You're sillier than I thought. This is a seven-day wonder: here today, gone tomorrow.

Time will tell. But in the meantime, it's me talking this through with you. I was saying that I learned to make people laugh.

So what? You're the wacky weirdo here. What's the point?

Prior to my laughter involvement, I led the yuppie life, preoccupied with making lots of money and climbing the social hierarchy. But as I learned under my guru, some strange and unpredictable things happened.

This is absurd! Kinkier than I thought. It's weird.

> *"Laughter is the brush that sweeps away the cobwebs of your heart."*
> —Mort Walker

Yes. Weird is the way things went. I thought my guru would teach me the mechanics, the bag of tricks of how to make people laugh. Instead, he focused on my anger and talked about compassion as the urge to bring laughter to people. I was shown how people ultimately want to love and be loved. I discovered how laughing with a stranger builds an instant emotional bond, a compelling, pervasive energy that fills up the atmosphere with positive vibes.

I get it. That must have been the mushy stuff that stole your soul away.

You're right. My soul was hooked. Before long, my soul in turn hooked me too, and now I'm in front of you, body and soul together. Whatever I now say goes for I, me, and myself as one entity.

You're obviously bewitched by this newfound toy. Do you make a lot of money out of it?

Oh, I don't earn any money from spreading laughter. On the contrary, I could be *spending* some of my own for it. I give my best efforts and energies, my time and resources to make people laugh. I've created a web site and get people over for a good laugh. I don't charge any money.

So the people who show up get a free ride. By golly, what a sucker you are!

My laughing participants have given me more than I can ever hope to repay. I seem to have found a reason for my existence, a connection with my calling. In a way, I've found *myself*.

Stop being so mushy-gushy. What do you specifically achieve by doing this, and what do your participants gain?

I dispel tensions and stress. I help people escape their frustrations and anger, their anguish and suffering from day-to-day grievances. I help in replacing melancholy and isolation with free-flowing laughter.

You call this your charity?

I do. Isn't this an act of helping, of healing?

You mean people actually fall for your childish gig? It's preposterous!

People travel great distances to take part in my laughter sessions. They don't call me silly or childish. On the contrary, they love the *gig*, as you say.

And do you love the gig as much?

I feel the unbridled joy of giving and sharing. My spirit and soul are spellbound by an intense feeling of satisfaction, and that's what rules my heart and all of me. I feel a great warm glow in my heart.

So this is your wow! It seems your guru—this laugh doctor—hypnotized you with his laughter.

I thought so too, initially, until I was totally bowled over by it.

I had viewed the road to success as money, name, and fame. But suddenly I saw myself making a U-turn. All my money-making machinations and the trappings of success began to seem small and superficial after I'd immersed my soul into spreading laughter. The way I feel in making people laugh is overwhelming, so entrancing and electrifying, more rewarding than anything else I've experienced before.

Hmm. I can see why your soul was swept away. Fickle things, souls.

That may be true. Once the laughter activity came into my life, my soul wanted no part of my social and professional ambitions, my deal-making. It returned to my heart only when I was spreading laughter. This is the biggest thing that excites and enthralls me and my soul now.

Cheap thrills.

Well, all the earlier thrills turned cheap: the things I'd earlier hankered for, the money, the possessions—they all seem trivial. The joy from the act of inducing and sharing laughter is a new realm of joy: heavenly, divine, almost Godly.

These two words—God and heaven—are the most worn-out clichés I've heard. Whatever you don't know or understand is God and heaven.

Oh, come on, Mr. D, it's a manner of speaking. I'm just describing the intensity of my feelings. I'm like one possessed.

Ah! That's a term I understand. I often take over and possess some human souls for my ends, evil as they are.

Your possession of human souls forces them to blindly do your evil bidding, but my soul possessed me with a passion to do good. It's as if my heart and spirit are taken over by the sheer rapture of what I do. I'm totally captivated by it.

I guess there are no limits to how ludicrous, how illogical and irrational you humans can be. Only a lunatic would throw away pots of money and all the goodies of life just to bray around like a jackass with strangers.

And that's exactly why I'm here, talking to you. At times I do feel as if I'm a lunatic. I put aside other pressing matters in my life just to make people laugh. Many people still scoff at me, and sometimes I wonder if I'm doing the right thing. Yet, deep inside me I'm still haunted by my conflicts, my impatience, and a fierce anger that comes and goes in flashes. Aren't these dual standards? Laughing at one moment, lamenting the next?

I'll address your conflict later. In the meantime, I still find it ludicrous that you feel uplifted by your synthetic, canned laughter. It's silly to elevate this tomfoolery to the heights you've taken it to. You think that your laughter is a fix-it-all!

Oh, my laughter participants may *fake* it to start with, but they *make* it to the real thing soon. So it's not canned at all. It's fresh and free-flowing.

And the laughter does come close to a fix-it-all. It cures both physical and mental illness and has great social benefits. I could list all the medical health benefits, but I'm not here to justify myself with evidence. I've actually *felt* all the evidence I need. During my laughter sessions, I've met with hundreds of people who couldn't thank me enough, who hugged me, who laughed till they cried. I feel wonderful to have brought them to it.

> *"Laughter is the closest distance between two people."*
>
> —Victor Borge

Laughed till they cried?

I have a collection of hundreds of real-life experiences from real people: the stressed stockbroker who cured his sleeplessness; the stiff and stodgy office worker who had forgotten how to smile but regained her zest; the drug addict who felt that life was worth living after all and took up a plan of rehabilitation; and the suicidal lady who laughed and cured her depression.

You're kidding!

Most of my participants are repeat visitors. They come for a good laugh and to share their experiences of how the light-headedness makes them forget

> *"Against the assault of laughter nothing can stand."*
>
> —Mark Twain

their worries, anxieties, angers, and frustrations. Some of the stories are real gems.

Such as?

I can recall at least two persons who benefited from the positivity of laughter and sent their cancer into remission. Then there's the case of the man who was suffering from the emotional turmoil of bereavement and, by laughing with us, lightened his burden. There is a regular to my laughter sessions who suffers from intense arthritic pain and travels a good hour so she can come "laugh it off," as she says. Finally, I know of a comatose lady who first twitched her eyes, then her fingers, then her feet, and finally began to walk when one of our laughter participants tried the technique on her.

That's incredible!

Let me tell you about one of our regulars, a ninety-three-year-old man who was wheeled in by his son. He could barely move a limb and hardly spoke, but

> *"You don't stop laughing because you grow old. You grow old because you stop laughing."*
>
> —Michael Pritchard

his eyes twinkled with our laughter. Eventually this man missed two sessions, and I wondered what happened. Lo and behold, he was back soon, but this time with a drip attached to his wheelchair, and connected to all sorts of tubes and wires. The son told me that even on his deathbed, his father had badgered and begged to be taken to my laughter session as a last wish.

I could see the old man's eyes light up as we laughed, and then very gently, very carefully, through all the tubes and things, I hugged him. That's when he shed a tear, and I shed several.

Whew! Are these experiences real?

Absolutely. An especially touching case concerns a lady in her late sixties. She visited my laughter session in Hong Kong a long time ago, but stood on the sidelines without participating. She refused to cooperate to our nudges to participate, to clap, to play and laugh.

It seemed as if her grim and angry visage was set in stone, eyes hawkish, brows knitted, forehead creased, and lips drawn tightly shut.

I was embarrassed with my inability to draw her out of her obvious animosity and so I thought, well, win some, lose some.

Surprisingly, the lady showed up again. Then again. Same posture, same embittered look, as if sneering at the rest of us merrymakers with scorn. I felt it improper to banish her but was uneasy with the question of why she bothered to attend in the first place.

And then, at the end of her third attendance, when everybody had left, I noticed that she stayed back. I made a sheepish attempt to address her concerns. That's when the dam burst!

What dam?

She burst into tears and began sobbing uncontrollably. She hugged me and said, "Bless you, my son." She broke down completely as I offered her some tissues and sat down next to her.

Hmm. Then what happened?

I tried my best to comfort her, knowing well that I had just witnessed a great catharsis—a release of pent-up emotions. I did not ask for an explanation, and she did not volunteer any as she continued to hug me.

And then what happened?

In a few minutes, she regained her composure, did not say a word, and left. Walked out of my life.

> *"Remember, men need laughter sometimes more than food."*
> —Anna Fellows Johnston

Forever?

Or so I thought. In truth, I migrated to the United States and left the running of the laughter group to another leader I had trained. On a casual visit to Hong Kong a year later, I dropped into the laughter class and there she was. Clapping, laughing, animated. The sparkle in her eyes as she glanced at me is seared into my memory forever.

Just one glance from her said it all. Greeting, gratitude, applause, love, praise, and the rapport of a special bond all rolled into one.

No logic can explain this.

This is the logic of *feelings*. They take you to where you're comforted. The angry, lonely, and depressed—they turn up, time after time, with amazing punctuality. It's clear that what pulls them over is an atmosphere where people are just plain happy, where there is a chance to touch your inner heart.

Are you touting the benefits of laughter to me?

No, not really. This dialogue between us is not about what laughter does for others but what it does for me. I feel as if I'm releasing people from some kind of bondage, stopping all confusion and negativity dead in its tracks. To me, laughter is a surefire way to cut through the clutter and warm my heart. The end result is an enigma—because this process of liberating others somehow works to liberate me too.

Is this a lecture on all the great things that laughter does, for the world and you?

Sorry to get carried away, Mr. D. My point is about how and why making people laugh has transformed my life.

When and where did you get this feeling first?

Let me put it this way: I went in for laughter training on a whim. Maybe the subconscious motive was to find my tongue. Learning a few moves wasn't enough to cure my inarticulate shyness. I remained tongue-tied and terrified. Can you guess what cured me of my nervousness on my opening night, when I led a laughter group of seventy-five people?

No. Maybe a few stiff drinks?

That's a good one! But jokes aside, as I bumbled my way to begin the laughter session, I felt some higher force urging me on. Once I looked upon my laughter class as an act of helping and healing, the rapture of this higher purpose took over. I forgot all my shyness and clumsiness. As my heart became intent on doing good for those I laughed with, it was as if God from up above put the right words into my mouth and guided me through the right moves.

A great transformation happened within me. As I tasted the gush and glow that surrounded me, my courage knew no bounds. Gone was my shy, sheepish, shrinking, and stuttering self. Some mystic, bigger energy had taken over, defying the odds and filling me up with confidence.

I know the feeling. Same as when I'm moving in for the kill. I, too, feel transformed, deaf to the cries and wails that abound when I wreck and ruin.

You're you, Mr. D, and I'm me. The act of spreading laughter made me come alive to a purpose of my existence. What began as a way out of my self-conscious shyness turned out to be something far bigger!

But your laughter's not natural. You said so yourself. It's induced, artificial, put on. It's a silly game!

I don't know if it's silly or unnatural. If you ask me, it's humor that's unnatural. Children laugh so easily and frequently and don't need humor or jokes. Only we adults, numbed with the challenges of life need humor as a trigger. *The Wall Street Journal* cites field research on the streets and malls and concludes that most laughter has little to do with humor. It's an instinctual survival tool for social animals. Laughter is a signal to be friendly, not an intellectual response to wit. The ones who laugh readily are the sociable, friendly ones. It's not about getting the joke; it's about getting along.

Ha! Are you recommending laughter as a do-it-yourself thing? You must be crazy—that's not the way respectable humans laugh and celebrate.

The ability to make people laugh has given me a new attitude toward life. I seem to have discovered a new energy within myself. A new excitement.

There's no need to snowball me with this sicko story! But I'm curious about what led you into this absurd activity. Tell me a bit about your background, yourself.

I was born into an elite household in India with a relatively charmed upbringing. My parents were loving and supportive, with strong and noble moral values. And an equally forceful achievement orientation to match.

I'm lucky to have received a good education that gave my career a good start.

That doesn't explain the source of your charitable leaning.

Oh, I witnessed firsthand the abject poverty so prevalent in the India of the sixties. I couldn't help but notice thousands of less fortunate urchins of my own age, clothed in rags, barefoot and ill-fed. Many worked as day laborers. In our own house, the children of our domestic servants helped with the chores, all for the leftover scraps of food.

Even before I reached my teens, I couldn't help being haunted by their hungry, hapless situation. I couldn't help wondering, "What if our roles were reversed?"

So you were moved by the plight of those less fortunate than you?

You could say so. And my mother is especially charitable and religious. I'm inspired by her compassion in so many ways.

And you followed your soul into this charitable grounding?

It's probably more correct to say that within me lay my dormant soul, which tagged along for the ride well into my material success in life. But it lay in wait for an opportunity to rediscover, renew, and relive its compassionate grounding. And at the right time, I was the one tagging along with my soul, doing its bidding.

> *"Man alone suffers so excru-ciatingly in the world that he was compelled to invent laughter."*
> —Nietzsche

Hmm. Did you realize your ambitions in life? Achieve whatever you wanted to, and become whatever you dreamed of?

Yes and no. Yes because the work I do has earned me financial security beyond my dreams. No because I could have done so much more.

The issue here is that having gotten to where I was at the age of fifty, I felt stagnant, emotionally and spiritually. And when your spiritual side is not firing at full pep, the soul wanders, like mine did. It was either stolen by laughteryoga or stole itself away from me to find its food elsewhere.

And your laughter enterprise was the food of your soul?

I guess so. In retrospect, this is the *spiritual anchor* that it provided to me, so that I could give vent to my natural effervescence. My gusto for life.

Oh! You're probably a bumpkin, a simpleton who doesn't know how to enjoy life to the full. Come on, there are a zillion ways to whet your appetite on the goodies of life.

I'm sure there are. Most of these I'd already tasted when I chanced upon laughteryoga, but there's really no end to how much food and drink you can consume. Or how much pleasure you can experience.

What's wrong with living the perfectly normal life of pursuing pleasure? From up above where I soar over you mortals, I can see lots of smug and contented people rejoicing in their revelry, inundated with indulgence. I don't see their need for a spiritual anchor as you say. They eat and drink and have sex. In fact, nothing beats a good sexual orgasm. It surpasses all your silly squawking about such soppy stuff.

Sex is indeed one of the most powerfully wonderful experiences that God has gifted us. Please don't misunderstand. I'm not for a minute saying that I'm into some self-denial trip, or dabbling with asceticism. I still enjoy my evening drink and my sex and my appetite for life's goodies. The deep release, the inner joy I feel when I'm laughing with my group—it's almost orgasmic.

Ha! How can you compare the reach and depth of a sexual orgasm with your ho-ho, ha-ha fooling around?

> "Laughter and orgasm are great bedfellows."
> —John Callahan

Laughter is equally powerful, Mr. D. In both hearty laughter and sexual orgasm, there is a release of energy rushing through the mental, physical, and emotional body. You've lost control of yourself. Sometimes when you're really, really laughing, your whole body starts tingling. That's a *gigglegasm*. Some people laugh, others cry, during intense sexual orgasm because of the deep cathartic experience. Similarly, during laughter, some people laugh till tears come.

Ha! Would you rather laugh than have sex?

I'd have both. Why can't I enjoy my sex and enjoy my laughs too?

You're obviously enchanted by spreading laughter. Personally, I can think of a million better things to do. I don't get it. What moved you to this senseless stupidity? Were you not content with your life when you took this on?

Oh, I was doing fine before this laughter overwhelmed me. My life was going great guns, both professionally and socially. I was the envy of my peers. That's when my soul parted company from me. You know what happened next, and the upshot is the here and now. In scattering laughter, I've discovered a purpose to my life.

A purpose? What's wrong with a plain, hassle-free life? What purpose can there be in your weird and kooky urge to make people laugh? I don't see the logic of spending so many resources on this petty pursuit. You don't get even a cent back.

What I get back is more valuable to me than money. I feel as if I'm healing people, drawing them away from their anger, despair, and depression, and this feeling is priceless! Spreading laughter has infiltrated my life.

Surely you can find something more normal to do! Use your imagination! You humans are capable of exceeding your physical limits. Your history is full of mighty warriors, great leaders, artists, achievers, and famous people. Why did you choose this idiocy?

I can't say I was born with artistic talent, or some other gift. And I don't have the grit and zeal of great men.

I'm just an insignificant nobody who wants to tuck into the greatest joys of life. In making people laugh, I've found the deepest joy I know.

Stop looking at me with that glazed, glassy look. You're obviously bewitched by what you do, enchanted with this penchant.

That's right! It's a wondrous rapture I feel, a great elation and happiness that's difficult to describe. When I make people laugh, in a way I'm freeing them from the harshness of life's struggles. It's like giving them a respite, like an oasis, from the seriousness and gravity of their existence. I feel a great gush of goodness oozing out of me, and the feeling's fabulous.

If you're so taken in by your laughter and so smug and enraptured by yourself, then why summon me?

I need to reconcile my sympathetic persona with my scornful, sneering feelings of skepticism toward people who don't care for courtesy or consideration.

Aha! So your laughter is not a cure-all!

It means a lot to me, but I still harbor my apprehensions and my inner turmoil. I'd appreciate your views on my innate intolerance and impatience.

I'll address your concerns shortly. In the meantime, these superlatives you use are sickening. Even more laughable is your preoccupation with laughing. If you must, there are tons of other ways to vent your energy. Why must you make an ass of yourself in public with your tomfoolery and horseplay?

I feel like a healer, a savior of people, by busting their anxieties, leading them by the finger away from their dark clouds and into the sunny emotions of love, hope, and joy.

How can I deny myself the intense joy, the euphoria that I feel in both laughing and making others laugh? For me, this is the pinnacle of pleasure.

> *"He deserves Paradise who makes his companions laugh."*
> —Koran

What makes you sure that others respect you for what you do?

I'm sure because so many come to me as strangers and part as friends. The look in their eyes is one of deep appreciation and rapture. I'm admired and hugged. Many of my participants single me out and wish to train, to emulate what I do. And there are so many living examples of grateful people who openly admit that I've made a profoundly positive difference to their lives.

And yet there are umpteen less silly ways to make a difference.

Each to his own! Look, I respect everybody who lives a prim and proper life. My way of giving back just happens to be more offbeat.

This is laughable.

Laughable, or *laudable?*

What matters is that I enjoy making people laugh. It's given me confidence and a reason to live, a purpose. It's my way of making that little difference, of being in sync with God's great game plan. The joy I experience compels me to feel as if I'm enjoying some sort of *last laugh* in the journey of life.

Ha! According to Confucius, "man who laugh last not get joke."

It doesn't matter. What matters to me is that "he who laughs, lasts."

> *"He who laughs, lasts!"*
>   —Mary Pettibone Poole

VARIETY

CHAPTER 3

THE GETTING OF GIVING

 Your soppy, syrupy spiel on laughter doesn't impress me. As the devil, I'm not into your gleeful geekiness. You're beginning to test my patience.

 Oh, please, sir! You promised to hear me out. And I'm also patiently awaiting your comments on my original concerns: my skepticism and self-doubt.

All in good time. In the meantime, you've painted a nice, rosy picture about laughter and what it means to you. Can you think of the specific underlying reasons about why you're so taken up by this?

You read my mind! I'm bubbling over to talk about it with you. It's a subject I've researched to try and understand my feelings. You see, there's this strange, funny feeling I get whenever I do a good deed.

What! Another slobbery sermon?

I'm just describing my feelings. It's a sort of "warm glow" I feel inside my heart whenever I've done something to please or help anybody.

A warm glow in your heart? Like heartburn?

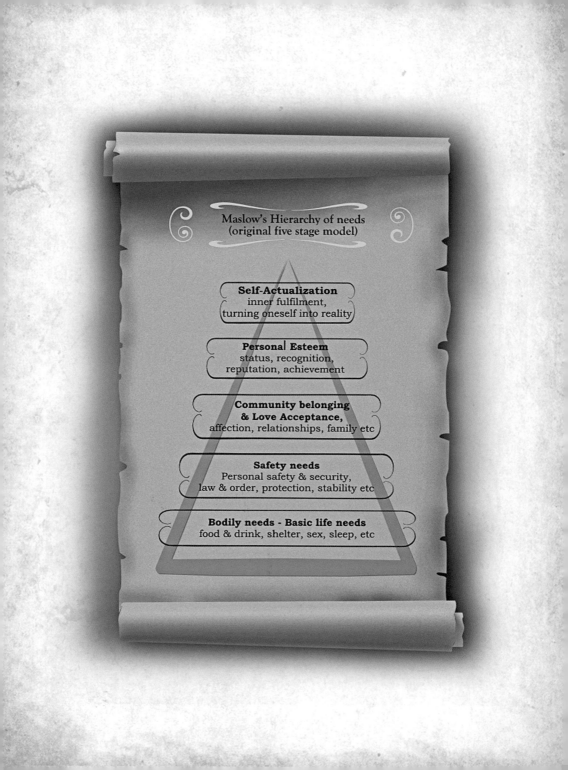

Quite the opposite. It's a peaceful, sweet feeling that sets my heart alight.

It's nothing to be excited about. Your social scientists have known it for centuries. The warm glow theory's about the internal satisfaction you humans feel when you give. Just think of it as a natural failing, another shortcoming of your cowering, cowardly human nature.

Just because other humans feel it doesn't make it any less precious. Whenever I've given my time to help anybody, or made a contribution of any sort, I'm filled with this wondrous inner light, a kind of total purity. Like a tingling sensation of warmth and love has entered my heart.

Enough of this poetic prattling!

Dear me, sir. I'm just describing the way I feel. And come on, Mr. D—you may not care much for our human failings, but you're the be-all, know-all for me. All I'm asking is that you hear me out.

Who's stopping you? Ask, just don't rant.

My life as a kid was a time of discovery and play, and in my youth I was busy chasing money and career. Success brought a buzz and boost to my ego, and I still work hard to earn my keep. But this warm glow, this great joy from helping and giving seems to have taken over my life. The feeling is so overpowering that it's overtaken other priorities. As I said, it's seduced and stolen my soul.

It's the "do-gooder" feeling: hollow and hypocritical to the core. And are you still raving on about your laughteryoga, or is this something new?

I'm describing the joy from the act of *giving*—any sort of giving—which produces a warm glow in our hearts.

You humans are so fickle and fallible! You can't seem to leave a good thing alone, can you? Look at it this way: your Abraham Maslow had this theory about the hierarchy of needs. You're animals to start with and your first need is survival: food and water, then safety and security. From my point of view, then it's savagery and sadism, but we're talking about you humans, not us demons.

Anyway, you then get into politics. That means you thirst for power, respect, esteem. This is nothing but a convoluted higher form of plain and simple greed. The warm glow feeling you've talked about is the same rush of blood that power brings. You need to be respected and admired, and so you sprinkle your fake help and spill a few crumbs around…

No, sir! I've read about Maslow too. After the primal survival and material needs are met, I guess man begins to want more. Power and politics is certainly higher up the ladder. Another name for this is *ego satisfaction*, when we want to hold others in sway. At the peak of the pyramid, Maslow talked about the need for self-actualization, though I'm not clear what this means.

I think that money or power do give a pleasurable boost, but of a different sort. The feelings from the act of giving are of a different dimension. The intensity is stronger and they last longer, yielding a kind of peaceful calm.

I'm bulldozed by this immense force. A great sense of wonder and fulfillment envelops me whenever I give my time or money toward a socially good cause. I'm not a wealthy man, though I've earned some tidy sums in my life. For some inexplicable reason, the thrill of earning and enjoying more money seems to have faded, taken second place to the great solace and satisfaction I feel from the act of giving. I want to dig deeper into myself to understand this feeling.

You want a spade to go digging?

Yes! And you're going to be my spade, Mr. D.

My dear chap, you've got it all wrong. You can dig and dig, but all you'll find is rocks and rubble. Your pretense about helping and giving is about one-upmanship and social clout. Basically, you humans descended from animals, and the first and foremost instinct of all animals is to hunt and hoard—to become king of the jungle and have all the other animals cowering in awe.

You're probably right, but that would apply to animals, not thinking humans. I've spent some time researching the why and how of this "warm glow." In the early days of psychology, people turned to Sigmund Freud for an answer to how and why the act of giving produced pleasurable sensations—a fact later confirmed by his daughter Anna Freud.

I suppose you're right that most of the time our reactions do follow the "fight or flight" syndrome for which all animals, including humans, are hardwired. It's an attitude based on instinctive animal reaction and becomes our lifestyle. We face it, fight it, or flee from it.

The concern I'd like to discuss with you is when we humans rise above our animal origins and look upon life with righteousness and love. When our survival needs are met, we don't *have* to lead an animal's predatory life and can look beyond the veil of fear at new vistas for understanding and appreciating life.

Your lovie-dovie-givie actions are just a ploy to lord over your fellow humans. Quite an effective tool to bowl over the weaker ones and have them eating out of your hand. Your talk about finding some deranged enjoyment beyond your survival needs—it's hogwash! Your underlying instinct is to chase and devour.

But there are a lot of research findings about how a compassionate, giving, and forgiving attitude yields amazing psychological and physical health benefits.

Research, schmesearch—all bunkum! They'll twist the facts till they have you around their little finger!

But these are all proven research studies. The first is a survey by Michael Steger, a psychologist at the University of Louisville

> *"Remember that the happiest people are not those getting more, but those giving more."*
> —H. Jackson Brown

in Kentucky. He observed that the more people participated in helping others, listening to others' problems, or pursuing one's life goals, the happier they were. Pleasure-seeking behavior did not make people happier. In a paradoxical way, giving gets you more than getting things for yourself.

Your helping and giving is selfishly oriented. This is a subtle move. Beneath the helping exterior, it's a power play. Power ploy is a better word. On the surface, it makes your chest swell out, but lurking behind this is your selfish interest. You humans are good at playing games with yourselves!

I don't deny that we humans can fool ourselves, and that we do have selfish motives. But the evidence points to how helping others in some way gives us a good feeling and a great sense of satisfaction, which exceeds the gratification of getting things for ourselves.

Don't play with words! Only your human sentimentalism is capable of all this mushy stuff. Your inborn and innate motive is the lust for power so you can surround yourself with gawkers.

There's another study done by Columbia University. It concludes that doing good deeds causes a rise in dopamine and other brain chemicals known to boost the mood. Our motives for giving really don't matter, but the more you give of your time or money to worthy causes, the more happiness you get.

I don't care what boosts your brain chemicals. Your motive is what counts. It's conniving and crafty to the core!

I'm a living example of the warm fuzzy feeling humans get when doing a good deed. You put it down to an ugly, ulterior motive, but that's not true. On the contrary, I believe you have to have a big heart to give away your comfort, your money, your time, your position—to do an anonymous good deed. And there's an opportunity cost too, because the same time could be spent chalking up a bigger paycheck or a promotion or just plain old good times. We humans can be dumb, but not so miserably dumb.

You don't seem to understand. Your genes were brainwashed a few thousand years ago by the religious brigade. Every religion encourages giving and suggests how you'll be saved by doing it! Your warm, mushy-gushy feeling is really due to religious programming. It's the goody-goody feeling you experience in "serving" the Lord.

Religion is so deeply encoded into your value system that it's crept into your instinctive reactions. The flush and flutter you feel isn't from giving but from observing and obeying your orthodox religion.

I can't say I'm very religious, but I do enjoy this great gush from giving. You, too, have recognized the existence of this emotion.

I'm not denying that the feeling exists. I'm questioning your motives. You give to feel like the flowery do-gooder, full of self-righteousness and importance. If anything, it's a higher form of consumption and simply pumps up your ego.

You've ascribed an ulterior motive to the act of giving. Maybe that's right, because doing good deeds is good for our physical health. Allan Luks, in his book *The Healing Power of Doing Good*, describes the results of a three thousand participant survey at more than twenty organizations. He saw a clear cause-and-effect relationship between helping and good health, and concluded that "helping contributes to the maintenance of good health, and it can diminish the effect of diseases and disorders, both serious and minor, psychological and physical." The volunteers in Luks's study testified to feeling a rush of euphoria, then a longer period of calm after doing a good deed. Luks called it the *helper's high*: a sharp reduction in stress and the release of endorphins. You get a great rush, or gush, of improved physical and emotional well-being from doing a good deed.

Whoa! Don't you love playing the pompous professor!

> "If you haven't got any charity in your heart, you have the worst kind of heart trouble."
>
> —Bob Hope

Stress is the root cause of hundreds of ailments, including obesity, acidity, hypertension, and sleeplessness. If we can learn to handle stress, then more than half of our physical and mental problems vanish. A drop in stress helps asthma, arthritis, and depression patients to vastly relieve their condition. Ninety-five percent of Luks's respondents who experienced the "helper's high" rated their health as better than others of the same age. Exactly how this works is perhaps related to the why and how our immune system gets strengthened. Giving helps you de-stress and decrease the intensity and awareness of pain. It reduces hostility and the negative emotions that damage the body. On the other hand, it activates emotions that enhance good health.

These are all fake conclusions. Oh sure, stress is a great killer of your fragile bodies, but you're the people who pile it on thick. Besides, you can't label your giving as the be-all and end-all of your problems. The people who give aren't exactly your Rambo-type stressed-out sods. On the contrary, they're the picture of peaceful piety, content to start with. You can't credit your results to giving—these results are blurred by hundreds of other reasons.

That may be so, but there's a strong connection between giving and good health. A ten-year study of the physical, health, and social activities of 2,700 men in Michigan found that those who did regular volunteer work had death rates two and half times lower than those who didn't And Dan Baker, in his famous bestseller *What Happy People Know*, quotes various studies which conclude that the happiest people are those who help others and donate to worthy causes. Then again, psychiatrist George Vaillant in his 1977 book *Adaptation to Life* describes his thirty-year study of Harvard graduates. Here, he concluded that adopting an altruistic lifestyle is a critical component of mental health—

Enough of this lecturing! You've glorified the notion of altruism beyond reason. I'm sure this works—who's denying it? But if you think it's the health draw that pulls people into doing good deeds, then you're sadly mistaken. It's the health scare that gets you humans going.

I'm not saying that the health advantage is the *reason* why people pursue altruism. I think it's the involuntary by-product of doing good deeds.

So what's the cause? Stupidity?

Come on, Mr. D, you've got a negative view about everything.

Isn't that why you drew me into this talk?

Okay—let's try another motive for why people perform good deeds. A wise man once said that you may amass great wealth and power in life, but in the end you can't *take it with you*. However, you *can* take a good deed with you.

Where? Upstairs? To heaven or to hell? You'll become fertilizer one day, so what's the chance your "good deed" will stay with you? Your concept of the afterlife is based on religious heresy. So why shoot for something that can't be seen? Has no evidence?

I can't put my finger on it. But I do believe in a heaven and a hell. I think if we do good deeds on earth, we'll reap the rewards in heaven.

Looks like you're already cramming for your finals!

Oh no, I think my finals will come after a few more decades—at least I hope so.

Your reference to heaven comes from your chirrupy churchmen. It seems you're too influenced by religion and its call for charity. Your story of heaven and hell is part of your religious conditioning, a term they've hatched to seize your fickle imagination and hold you in check.

I used the word as I've been taught to describe the rewards that await us after we're dead and gone. But even right here during our living years on earth there are great rewards for doing good deeds. You stay healthier, you sleep better, people love you and respect you, and you get this great high, a great elation, a high that beats booze, beats drugs—

Sure doesn't beat sex!

The sexual act culminates in a great whoosh, but we humans need a rich variety and depth of gratification. Sex is only one of these. There's something unique about the joy from doing the right thing, the good thing, the sacrificial thing. There is by now evidence from hundreds of research papers about how social connectedness and giving not only produce pleasurable sensations in us but actually improve our health.

In the magazine *Psychology Today*, heart specialist Dr. Herbert Benson has reported how amazing health benefits can be found from the act of altruism, just as with yoga, spirituality, and meditation.

You're bleating on and on about the benefits of giving. Ever try some pills or yoga or meditation or biofeedback? Or knocking off some of that big tub around your waist? You can't whine on about altruism as the ultimate cure for all your ills.

Can we just say that altruism is a kind of yoga or meditation or spirituality?

Not so fast, kiddo! You can be one and not the other. A hard-core crook from the mafia can also find certain calming and health benefits from yoga and meditation. Vice versa, you can have a doddering old confused do-gooder who's performing altruistic activities, but knows nothing of yoga and meditation. Both experience some sort of elation, a kind of high.

So what's the big deal about your altruistic "helper's high" when you can get an equally good runner's high or politician's high or sexual orgasm high. Or the one that meditators and yogis enjoy. A high is a kind of climax of joy that you can enjoy from a variety of activities. Your warm glow high is just one of the many forms of elation you can enjoy.

My warm glow high is higher than the other highs, and deeper too, and more long-lasting. I do believe that altruism gives the same kind of health benefits as yoga and meditation, but for sheer joy and emotional satisfaction, you can't beat the warm glow from giving.

Altruism is not for the common man, not for all of you.

We're talking about some very serious money that is given as altruism to charity every year. For the year 2006, almost 70 percent of all households in America gave some $300 billion, or around 2 percent of their GNP. Surely there's *something* that drives these people to donate such large sums?

Pure, old-fashioned greed. Selfishness. Pursued through politics. If it's not the plain politics of "me first" and "me big," then it's a political agenda of "this first" and "this big." The balance reasons are to do with tax benefits, religious faith, social popularity, and control—plain old showing off. A good slice of that $300 billion you spoke of comes from bequests and foundations. That's the super-rich buying into sympathy and adulation, or telling your God upstairs, "Hey, I'm on the way—save your best for me!" They're hoping some of it will trickle down into the afterlife, or into rebirth.

Then sometimes you fickle humans dig into your pockets whenever there's a natural disaster somewhere. This is guilt trip giving. Often, those of you who've made it big look down from your fortresses at the slaving worker ants. To assuage your guilt, you shower a few bucks.

Bill Gates didn't just shower a few bucks. Neither did Warren Buffet or Andrew Carnegie or a long list of wealthy philanthropists. These people gave most of what they had. You can't discredit their noble gesture.

Noble? From the look on your gaping, gawking mouth, I can see you dreaming of their billions. The point is—what option did they have? Over the past hundred years, your family system of values has eroded, filial bonding has corroded. If you're super-rich, there's only so much you can eat and consume. So you want to hit the headlines, make a big splash. There's no way you can spend all that dough, and your kids certainly don't deserve it. So you do the one thing that makes you become God on earth. You give left, right, and center so you're always in the news. And silly suckers look up in awe and treat you like some saint.

> *"Happiness comes from spiritual wealth, not material wealth... Happiness comes from giving, not getting. If we try hard to bring happiness to others, we cannot stop it from coming to us also. To get joy, we must give it, and to keep joy, we must scatter it."*
>
> —John Templeton

There is now a new brood of people who donate far beyond their means. This is called *stretch* giving. A washerwoman during her active lifetime gave $150,000 to the University of Mississippi. Dr. Doty at the age of fifty-one gave away $28 million, or 99 percent of his net worth, to an HIV program. There are more living examples, and the numbers keep growing every year. The giving may not be money, but volunteerism. Such as how Mary Shalo continued to do volunteer work for the Red Cross and various other societies from 1940 all the way to the ripe age of eighty-nine. I wonder what makes such people tick?

Silly, senseless stupidity. What other reason could there be?

Come on, Mr. D—I think people are altruistic chiefly for the good feelings this brings about. How else do you justify the actions of the millions who donate generously? I'm sure there's *anonymous* giving going around too. Like Chuck Feeney whose giving since 1982 has exceeded $4 billion. Chuck takes pains to disguise his identity, travels coach or economy class, and rides the subway. His kids worked summers as waiters, hotel maids, and cashiers. What could be the possible reason for that?

Your human brains can be fickle, illogical, and unreasonable. A behavioral economist, Ernest Fehr of the University of Zurich in Switzerland, says it better than me: "None of our current theories can explain altruism when there is anonymity and therefore no chance of reciprocity or enhancing your reputation."

But the same Ernest Fehr says that "human altruism is unique in the animal world," meaning that it exists and abounds even whilst defying an explanation. At churches you do sometimes find people pulling out the big notes. And history does have records of people who—

Threw it out of a helicopter? Ha-ha!

Look, it's hard to give you cold, hard reasons other than what we humans have: *feelings*. I'm the human here, and I'm describing what *I feel*.

Most of your reasons for giving are selfish. Often, you give to save embarrassment. Take your own church contribution example: if Peter pulls out a tenner, then Paul looks bad with anything less. The rich often get so full of themselves that they forget their human frailties. They want to feel powerful and play God. So they give to where they can exercise social control. Your typical Mr. Rich-n-Famous often gives to the museum or university that dons his name. The intention is to have people sit around in awe.

Sometimes it's to remember your dead. You stick up a big pillar for the departed dead so you can show the world how you've cried!

Stop it! You may never have experienced love, Mr. D, but we humans believe it's all there is, a reason to live. So what if people give in memory of the departed? At least they *give*. That's what counts.

You're quoting the research that supports your views, but I'm stating the cold facts. Often you give to define your character, to be able to say "that's who I am, and that's not who I am." It's why a guilty tax thief may give. Or somebody who's subjected to racial prejudice as a kid may give to this cause in later life. Or maybe the giving's done to impress somebody. A good fund-raising gimmick is to raffle off some cheap stuff at high-profile dinner galas for ridiculous prices. So the suckers who buy can get their moment of glory, bidding to beat their cronies by a display of put-on generosity.

The latest fad is giving circles. These are mostly ladies groups engaged in meaningless social chitchat masquerading as philanthropy with the message "see how meaningful we are."

Please. In spite of all the ulterior motives for giving, I'm the human here and you're not. So it's about how *I* feel, or *we humans* feel when we perform good deeds. I can't buy into your reasoning that the rich just shower their wealth around because they can. You can't deny that there's a purifying, rich, warm glow that bathes us when we give of our time or money to a worthy cause.

Again you're bringing up that corny "warm glow"?

It's not corny to me. It's good-heartedness. And oh—I guess that's why it's good for the heart! It gives me great joy and jubilation. In helping and giving, I feel good about myself, and when I feel good about myself, I feel good about the world. So I'm on more comfortable, peaceful, happier terms with the world and don't gripe about its whims. Many of us happily volunteer for causes we believe in. Some of our brave soldiers actively volunteer for the toughest spots in Iraq. They want to *give* toward what they believe in.

So many psychological studies have proven what I'm saying. I'm not here to say *why*, but to

> *"We make a living by what we get, but we make a life by what we give."*
> —Winston Churchill

describe what *is*. Our good deeds are followed by feelings of joy and satisfaction, whilst wicked actions produce shame and fear in us.

Y-a-w-n. I think a bug or virus has infected you, taken you over.

Yes! It's like a virus all right. When you're giving, then nothing else counts. Like a virus, this feeling is so overwhelming, so commanding that it spreads to every part of your life. In a way, you're hijacked.

Did you see the movie *Schindler's List*? This is a true historic portrayal of the Jewish persecution at the hands of the Nazis. The German onlooker Schindler led the perfectly normal, hedonistic, and pleasure-soaked life, until he was moved by the plight of the Jews and what they suffered at the hands of his compatriots. Almost by accident, Schindler discovered the joy of helping the Jews, saving them from the Nazis. At first he couldn't understand it, but soon his every thought, every action was directed toward one more good deed, saving one more life. Schindler took on great risks to help and rescue the Jews. Driven by this strange power from doing good, nothing else seemed to matter anymore to him.

And this seems to matter a lot to you.

Yes, it does. The giving bug bit Schindler and took over his life. I suppose there comes a time when the commands of the heart overrule those of our minds. This feeling defies explanation, but it exists in all of us.

And I maintain that it's a fake garb to be and act the "do-gooder"—just so you can have all the gawkers and gapers around you.

Look, Mr. D, we give up our time, our money, we risk our lives, we embrace pain. For *what?* Believe me, this "be good, do good" formula works magic like no other. It's like a drug, and you get hooked on it over a period of time. The purifying, inner calm and peace, the sheer blissful welling up of the heart, is so very divine. It's as if you're one with God.

> "I have found that among its other benefits, giving liberates the soul of the giver."
>
> —Maya Angelou

You speak of God as the ultimate euphoria, like heaven.

It may not be heaven, but the feeling is heavenly!

You're right that after the basics are met, we humans *do* crave recognition and power. This ego trip turns into an ego trap for many of us because we love to play the whimsical dictator, reveling in the power.

But some of us do look beyond the trappings of wealth and power to do charitable things, helping things. The feelings this stirs up are calming and entrancing, almost magical. Unmatched by anything that power provides. The love and warmth that giving generates is therapeutic—cleansing us from inside. You're a different person when you learn to truly *give*. It beats any other feeling.

Wow! I'm impressed by your vocabulary! Since your giving has so filled you with euphoria, then why bother with me—the devil?

Oh, to reconcile the good feelings from giving with the bad ones from impatience, anger, guilt, and fear. That's why I sought you out.

I'll address that question soon. In the meantime, your mad, moonstruck infatuation with giving won't get you far. You're just a masochistic windbag full of silly notions that can only cause suffering.

According to you, altruism is egoism. You think people give only to reap ulterior benefits or to assuage guilt or to escape feeling the way poor people do. Empathy is about *feeling* the needs of others, understanding their plight. The way I define altruism is having a desire to give to, and to sympathize and empathize with the less fortunate. To have no motive of receiving anything back from the act of giving.

So you think Bill Gates weeps about the hungry kids in the world, or sits by in disease-ridden hospitals like Mother Theresa?

No, but the definitions are becoming clearer now. There's institutional philanthropy at one end, practiced by the likes of Buffet, Bill Gates, and other billionaires without their personal involvement. The other side is charity, which is a direct connection with kindness and sympathy expressed toward helping the needy. Charity is closer to the misery because those who perform direct charity gain a closer connection with the subjects of their giving. They reap the direct person-to-person rewards of gratitude. In a perfect world, you need both philanthropy and charity because one can't survive without the other. Both acts are altruistic.

Altruistic, or masochistic?

That's your view, Mr. D; you don't have a human heart. I may sound masochistic, but I'm fortunate. Just when I was beginning to gloat

> *"I think the great livers, the poeple who are fully self-actualizing and alive, are the great givers."*
>
> —Mark Victor Hansen

about my money and success, I chanced upon the great joys of giving. This wonderful inner joy is more rewarding, deeper than the temporary fix from splurging money and power. It's more satisfying and fulfilling.

Dost thou wish that I bow to thee, Oh Patron Saint of Giving?

Ha-ha! You certainly know how to be snarky!

What a relief that there aren't too many of you giving types around.

I wouldn't say that. The people who give are everywhere donating their time, money, or efforts to whatever social or humanitarian cause. I think it's paradoxical that the most intense feeling of joy that God created for us humans is so invisible, yet freely available to all. It's there in every corner as opportunities to help. You can be born in any race, rich or poor, at any age or physical condition and yet savor the joy of giving.

Give me some real-life examples of ordinary, everyday people.

Sure. I have a dear friend whose dad retired as a senior civil servant. He made some appropriate financial settlements on his kids right away and then kept a meager share of savings for himself, to "splurge" as he desired. Or so he told his surprised kids. He couldn't be stopped from buying a piano for the local blind school and then went on to sponsor the rehabilitation of amputees into active life. When questioned about his sanity, he said that he wanted to die with nothing left over other than the spectacles on his face.

Hmm…

A wealthy family friend threw herself into collecting donations for those orphaned during the 2004 tsunami and gave generously to this cause. She devotes a lot of her time and money to active charity and has set up a free-of-charge computer learning facility for underprivileged children in Sri Lanka.

Sri Lanka? Is that where she lives?

No, she lives in Dubai. She wasn't looking to get the credit or the adulation. She prefers to remain anonymous about her giving both in Dubai as well as in Sri Lanka.

This is ridiculous!

The stories don't end. I know of many relatively poor people who still give what they can to charity, or find time to volunteer in some way. These are real people in real life. What do you think motivates them to give so generously?

I think they're befooled by the kick of self-importance that giving provides. It's an urge to experience pride, or "power over." Your smallest can feel big when they give, and you call it humanitarianism. The warm glow that exists in you is motivated by the human failing of trying to be "me bigger, me better." I fail to see why you glorify and worship this shortcoming in your character. You are made to seize the most in life.

You're right, Mr. D. In seizing the most in life, we must seek out and pursue the most joy and happiness. When people give, it's to maximize this joy. In fact, a recent study by Harbaugh, Mayr, and Burghart wired up volunteers to MRI (Magnetic Resonance Imaging) machines to map how their brains lit up when they donated out of free choice. The study concluded that the act of donating for the public good is motivated both by pure altruism and the warm-glow incentive. So I guess humans have evolved from their animalistic origins and actually enjoy the act of giving.

There could be another reason for your giving. Like some sort of self-deprecating joy in letting go of the prized catch you've hunted.

Maybe that's so, but one way or the other, you've got to commend the feeling.

> *"He who obtains has little. He who scatters has much."*
> —Lao-Tzu

There's nothing to commend. You humans are just incorrigibly foolish and irrational. It's precisely why I'm around to fill you up with fear and guilt, to put you back on track with your animalism.

You're here to do what you must do, and I guess we humans will do what we must do too. My own giving is the gift of laughter, which I take pains to spread as widely and as effectively as possible. This may sound unconventional, but it still works for me and has uncovered new emotions. Even as I respond to your jibes, this chat is clarifying my mind bit by bit.

Clarifying your mind? Here I am, listening to your childish prattling with sealed lips.

Sealed lips? You asked so many questions!

Only cross questions, just as you asked me to pose. You started out with doubts about yourself, your exasperation with the world around you. You expressed a helplessness against the elements that come in your way, which your impotent rage cannot deal with. I can't understand what magic you've found in your talk with me, when you did most of the talking!

You forgot the cynicism and skepticism I've developed over the years, the suspicion that everybody is out to get me, or do me in.

Fear, suspicion, persecution—all these are no strangers to me. It's what I dole out daily.

I started out in life with the notion that you've got to suspect the worst. Go for and get the most.

An excellent motto. What's wrong with that?

The cross purpose of where I am today. Some years ago, I would pin an ulterior motive to those who were performing some sort of charity, or *giving* in some way. Now that I've felt the great gush from giving, I'm confused about my other role in life.

What role?

The opposite of my giving role. In my commercial life, I'm in the *getting* mode, negotiating the best deals. In real day-to-day life the mantra is aggression, pitching the promise for maximum gain. This is where I'm confused. Am I a fraud to do what I'm doing?

There are too many answers to your question, which must be put in the right setting of who and what you are. I'll make my comments once I've heard you out in full. In the meantime, I can see that you're tickled pink with yourself, with this newfound toy of giving.

This isn't a plaything for me, Mr. D. The euphoria from giving has made it possible for me to live with my own tormented self. It's brought me and my soul together into a common purpose. Giving is for me an act of redemption— a healing energy to mend my own open wounds of distrust for this world. I'm still not totally clear about the reasons, but in the meantime I've found this salve to my sorrow and suffering. I've discovered that there's more joy in the act of giving than in getting.

Make up your mind. Are you talking about giving or getting?

Both. It's all the same. I think the best getting *is* giving, because only by giving can you truly get!

> "*Continually give, continually gain.*"
> —Chinese proverb

CHAPTER 4

THE MEANING OF MEANING

 Hi, Mr. D. How're you doing?

Just breakfasted on a dozen fatal motor accidents, some falls, a few strokes. And my favorite is the snake bite. Not a bad way to start the day.

 You mean you did all that just for fun?

Fun? My dear chap, it's a way of life with me—nothing funny about it. Somebody's got to keep the streets clean, the system running, the garden weeded.

So you're the angel of death?

I outsource most of my work. I've trained others to torture and torment, but I join in for the ride sometimes. Look, are we talking about me or you here?

 Gosh! I'm just a bit taken aback with what makes your day.

I'm who I am. I must do as I do. You're who you are, so let's focus on your issues.

 A while ago, you said that any giving by us humans is selfishly driven.

That's the main motive. The other possible explanation is masochism, or just plain old silliness and stupidity.

There's another aspect to giving that I wish to discuss. I've discovered the magnetism of another motive, a bigger reason.

Or the lack of it. I'm sure it's equally unreasonable.

The act of giving inspires a warm glow and soothes, but there's a related motive that leads to an even more intense satisfaction. This is the mystery I'd like to talk over with you.

My way of solving mysteries is a brusque, abrupt conclusion. Your giving glow has no place in my work.

There are questions that haunt each one of us as we mature: Who am I? Where did I come from? Where am I going? What will become of me when I leave this earth?

This particular debate is so innately inconclusive that your biggest libraries are too small to hold all the answers. My advice is that you travel the road yourself to find your own unique answers. That way you can satisfy your questioning, searching, prying nature.

Hmm. What happens once we've satisfied our survival needs, survived the politics of power, and there's no leftover urge to conquer and control?

That never happens. Your ego will always win. You've got to feed it with money, power, position. Your urge to show off and to control others will always get the better of you.

You're probably right about where our ego can take us. But when we have our ego in check, the quandaries return. There's an inner calling in each of us to find and seek something higher in life—higher than simply feeding the ego.

And what might that be?

To reach into our hearts and address the *purpose* of our lives.

Purpose? What other purpose do you have than to live out your life span as you were meant to? Grow up, reproduce, eat, and be merry. Then one day keel over and die.

That's too simplistic. Humans are more than just ordinary animals. We're blessed with a brain and intelligence. There's a curiosity we all have—about how and where we figure in the grand design of creation. Surely there's a purpose to our lives.

Ha! All of you are slaves to your desires and passions. You're never content in life and crave for more and more. Your mania for one-upmanship has no end. That's the A to Z of your purpose.

I guess most of us do hanker for more and more: possessions, indulgences, power. I've read about diamond-studded cell phones and cars and wondered what meaning the owners find in these "super-toys."

Meaning? Didn't I say that your programming is essentially animalistic? Hunt and hoard, romp and chomp, survival of the fittest—that's the only meaning you need. The men want to crack the whip, and the women want to be the queen bee.

What about life's purpose? Some of us do dwell on this debate.

You've got to be kidding! Purpose? You're on the prowl out there, trying to make ends meet. When you're eyeing all the goodies that surround you, then will you brood on such arcane thoughts? You've got to seize what you can before others ride roughshod over you. Your natural herd instinct is to protect your turf and maximize your conquests.

Up to a point, yes, you're right. In fact, for most of us, life ends with these ends. But please, I wish to look beyond the goodies, beyond the pull of power.

Whether or not our basic needs are first satisfied, I do believe that many of us question the purpose of our existence. Often we

> *"Purpose is what gives life meaning."*
> —Charles Henry Parkhurst

experience feelings that we cannot define or understand, such as the golden glow from the act of giving. Such feelings direct us to define our role in nature and creation, to understand our purpose for being on earth. What is the meaning of our life?

The meaning of life is to be keen, lean, and mean.

I was hoping for some direction from you. I wonder what Maslow referred to when he talked of man's highest need as the one for self-actualization. I suppose when our primary desires are fulfilled, it's an urge to give a body to, and actualize, all that you stand for in life.

Like leave your mark on this world? With ego as the engine?

How else do you define Gandhi and what he stood for? He's one great man who could change the destiny of the world, who filled hearts with love and conquered the world without violence. Gandhi realized and therefore actualized himself ably and fully.

Gandhi had the biggest ego of his time. Not only was he personally masochistic, but sadistic too. He rode roughshod over the lives of his wife and kids and made them suffer endless pain and deprivation. Are you aware that his son was driven to drink and died a lonely death on the streets?

Powerful people have powerful personalities. I can't say why, but I'm beset with trying to understand purpose, and it's one of the reasons I sought you out. I've read up on this, and I'm fascinated by what Martin Seligman, the father of modern positive psychology, has to say. He points out three major components of happiness: **pleasure, commitment, and meaning**.

Seligman's research shows that the first, hedonism, or maximizing pleasure, is the least important cause of happiness. The search for coherence, or calling—composed of commitment to family, work, friends and society, and the urge to conquer the meaning of life—produces more lasting and inner happiness in people. Finally, if one can identify with a social objective bigger and higher than oneself, it gives direction and purpose to us. This focusing of efforts toward furthering a cause is the biggest source of satisfaction and happiness.

So your ultimate good is the search for purpose and meaning. Can you explain the meaning of this meaning that you hanker for?

The search for purpose, or meaning, is an urge in us to define our inner selves. To build on a skill or ability with commitment and give vent to our creativity. The higher realms of happiness are found when we try to lend a purpose to our lives. We experience a unique sense of achievement when we can refine a hobby or interest toward perfection. Likewise, we feel a great sense of belonging if in some way we feel we are useful to the community at large. This association with a higher purpose is very rewarding.

You're sure you're not a professor in real life?

No. Why do you ask?

You certainly act like one, pompous and preachy. If I wasn't so piqued by your problem, I wouldn't have the patience to proceed with this dialogue.

Oh, I don't mean to offend you. It's just that I researched the subject out of curiosity. I think that finding a meaning to our lives is very important to us.

Do you understand this can mean different things to different people?

I'm sure each of us has his own unique calling, a different route to reach the same end.

You ignoramus! Your very committed, focused jihadi, or suicide bomber, has a purpose too, and finds meaning in what he does. You can praise and proclaim your Mother Teresa as a saint, working tirelessly towards a bigger cause. Why not the suicide bomber who sacrifices his life for his version of a social objective bigger and higher than oneself?

In a way, you're right. Deepak Chopra's view is that terrorism isn't insanity—it grows out of the social conditions of poverty, oppression, dictatorship, and lack of life purpose and meaning. The recruiters of suicide bombers are clever people who understand this human trait: the pursuit of meaning. For this reason, these "talent scouts" of suicide bombers look for volunteers in people who nurse a grievance against life. There are rich pickings for the recruiters in lawless societies, where repression and oppression are rife. The promise is the instant high of association to a "bigger cause," with spiritual redemption as the reward. The spiritually weak get suckered by the suggestion that the sacrifice of their lives will improve those of others. It's the fulfillment of the ultimate purpose at the ultimate cost. It works almost like a sting operation.

> "Men never do evil so completely and cheerfully as when they do it from a religious conviction."
>
> —Pascal

I thought that most of these poor suckers blow themselves up because of religious faith. You can see how religion brainwashes you…

That's not right. The black tigers, or suicide squad, of the Tamil separatists in Sri Lanka have no religious agenda. But you could be right; religion does play a big role in motivating suicide bombers in the Middle East. I suppose it's because our religious upbringing takes over our minds and hearts completely. Either because of social and cultural pressure or otherwise, we're forced to support, even fight, for our religion.

Aha! So your suicide bombers feel that they're being Godly or saintly in some way by blowing themselves up?

Such is the power of purpose. For better or for worse. The true flowering of purpose is perforce related to bettering the lot of the world, but the actions that fulfill this purpose are subject to many points of view. I suppose suicide bombers have their own.

Or are taught a particular point of view. Through religion.

Let's not blame religion, which is our belief system. The fault lies in some of our power-hungry warmongers who find it easy to package hatred and revenge into religious edicts. I suppose the religious masters are aware of the power of man's thirst for purpose and meaning, and routinely use this knowledge for their own earthly ends.

Ah! I'm impressed. There's at least one area where you and I see eye-to-eye. In spite of this, I maintain that your search for meaning and doing good doesn't apply generally to all of you. Your species is still in the animalistic stage. You are born, you grow up, you procreate, you fool around a bit, but essentially you lead the worker ant's preprogrammed life of chasing food and fodder till you die.

That may be so for most of us, but you can't deny that we as humans are born with an overpowering urge to seek purpose and meaning in our lives.

An urge that religions pounce upon to give their own canned answers to who and what is man? Who and what is God? What is life and death? Finally, what is the relationship between these mysteries?

Your concerns about your past, present, and future are fully addressed by religions, and your holy books are full of gospels about how to live out your life. Religion sells because it claims to have all the answers.

And so, my dear chap, religion hijacks your search for meaning and hitches it to its own ends, which are the glorification and perpetration of the religion that you were born into. It's a great fix for your wanderlust, which is then harnessed to fit into religious agendas. Religion has instant answers to your search for meaning and a commitment to something bigger and higher than yourself—all that your Martin Seligman talks about.

> *"Religion is an illusion and it derives its strength from the fact that it falls in with our instinctual desires."*
>
> —Sigmund Freud

You mean our search for meaning is planted there by religion? That's not true!

Look at it in another way. Does your search for meaning lead you to religion, or does religion lead you to your search for meaning?

I guess religion helps us on the way to find meaning, not the other way around.

Why? Do you mean that you can't find meaning in life without the aid of religion?

I suppose you could. But religion does serve a very useful purpose by extending our inner search for purpose and meaning. It gives us a good grounding and points us to God, who helps reveal the purpose of our lives.

Ha! Your religions tout themselves as a one-stop shop for all the answers to the unknown. That's why they sell.

I'm quite comfortable with my religion, even if that's what points me to a search for meaning. It's a good place to start.

Yes, with ready answers to pin down your purpose in life, and plenty of priests to pontificate and point you to the right way—their right way.

You don't have to be sarcastic.

What if your definitions of purpose and meaning don't coincide with your religious teachings? Is a religious person necessarily better or carry more meaning in his life than an agnostic?

You could be right, but I was brought up to regard religion with reverence. I'm comfortable with that thought and have no reason to challenge my own religion or any other.

Religion has brainwashed you. The "goody-goody" feeling you get as an aftermath of a good deed is because you feel a convoluted sense of holiness and Godliness, exactly as dictated by your religion.

You seem to agree that we humans derive some deep gratification from being and doing good. The warm glow of this gratification becomes stronger and more lasting—like an inner flame—once we attach a purpose and meaning to our lives. Why does it matter whether religion points the way or we seek it on our own?

> *"Philosophy is questions that may never be answered. Religion is answers that may never be questioned."*
> —Author Unknown

It matters a great deal. Because your urge for meaning—that you describe in such rosy terms—is both planted and nursed by religion in order to throw you onto a track that best suits its ends.

What are these ends?

Getting you to attend their loud services and prayer meetings, which are in themselves acts of brainwashing; getting some money out of you too; perpetuation of the particular religion; social and political control to keep you mentally and spiritually enslaved. The worst end of religious leaders is to brainwash their subjects to further their political agendas.

You mean as with suicide bombers?

A good example. My question here is why your being and doing good must be colored by, or satisfy the prescription of, your religions, which are narrow-minded. Must you be part of this club to be and do good?

You may have a point there, though the subject of religion doesn't interest me. My focus is on the wonderful feelings associated with *meaning*. And here I want to quote from the teachings of the Nazi Camp survivor Victor Frankl.

Frankl quotes from firsthand experience the hopelessness of the imprisoned Jews in German camps. The victims endured one indignity after another and faced certain death. With this backdrop, Frankl discovered that man could either become bitter, uncaring, and resigned, or plug in to a higher faith based on finding *meaning*. In Auschwitz and other camps, Frankl saw abject inhumanity at its worst: the inmates starved, cold, and laboring, separated from loved ones and hope. However, as long as they could find a *reason* to live, they could find the will to survive. Some chose to live selfishly and fatalistically. Others chose to be optimistic, helping and loving those around them. This selfless attitude and action even in the face of insurmountable suffering became their *reason* to live. The feeling of giving, helping, and finding a purpose became a precious survival tool to live by, for those that chose this path. Surprisingly, these were the people who outlived their ordeal, not the bitter ones.

Frankl concluded that man can survive anything if he feels that his life has a purpose. This *meaning* is discovered by creating a work, doing a good deed, experiencing a human value firsthand, or by freely giving love.

Are you talking about survival tools in extreme situations, or rambling on about the meaning of life?

I'm talking about something that exceeds the temporary pleasures from sensory and ego-gratification. I'm talking about a guidance system

> *"Suffering ceases to be suffering at the moment it finds a meaning."*
> —Victor Frankl

that works better than religion. How it's important for man to log on to his calling and to recognize and understand his meaningful role in the world.

I think that if you've discovered your meaning of life, then you've found a great, deep joy and bliss. When you make a connection with your purpose, it satisfies more than pleasure and lasts longer. This is what Frankl understood by his study of suffering on a close, firsthand basis. He said that the search for meaning is the primary motive of our lives.

Your search for meaning is politically motivated. Humans get this thrill from being respected and admired, and will do whatever it takes to experience the adulation. You can drone on about finding a higher purpose, but all you actually want is to rule the roost and feel good about it.

I can only speak for myself, not the world at large. My own feelings when I touch upon purpose and meaning in life both overwhelm and exhilarate me. I can't understand why I feel cleansed, glowing, flowing.

Your view about the political benefits makes it seem ugly and selfish, but I don't care! My feelings are precious and purifying, an oasis from the day-to-day challenges of life. Frankl found that many of the mental challenges and frustrations people face are because they don't realize that their lives lack purpose. One of his studies showed that a group of drug abusers initially started to take drugs because they felt their lives were meaningless.

Meaning, schmeaning! You mortals need something to believe in to get your jollies. Your religions teach you to toe the line of their mindless chanting to feel "cleansed, pure, glowing, flowing." You puff up your chests with pride when you're in the grip of some religious lip service.

How gullible and naive you humans are! Simpletons.

Meaning certainly means a lot to *me*! My own work of giving and spreading laughter has opened up a purpose to my life. I feel a sense of belonging and connectedness to humanity and the world. I feel entranced, fulfilled and enriched in a strange manner. In finding my purpose, I feel alive and radiant, as if a great rapturous calm is bathing me. My heart wells up with the purest form of love I know. It's like being close to and one with God.

You've put the purpose of life on a pedestal. Ha! Do you think life gives a damn about your purpose?

I really don't care if anybody gives a damn. It's about how *I* feel. I've found gold with this discovery about how we humans tick. It brings a great relief from clutter and confusion, and lasting joy. I honestly feel that for those who can identify life purpose and meaning, there's no turning back to mundane matters.

Most of you on earth are more worried about the next meal, the next buck, the next conquest. You humans have stretched the meaning of survival to new heights. You need a new toy each day to entertain you. You're too preoccupied with today's luxuries, which are tomorrow's necessities. So when you praise your finding of meaning, then you speak for yourself—not the overall majority.

That's not true. Every day people seek meaning in their own way too. So many people living hand-to-mouth still find something to donate from their meager means. Or they volunteer their time for a cause they believe in. It's obviously to lend some meaning to their lives.

I recall an incident during my laughter sessions, when a bejeweled and wealthy lady asked me "Do you do parties?" Since I prefer to see myself as a spiritual guide rather than a commercial entertainer, I replied that I "did" parties, but on a selective basis and not for money. She couldn't understand why, but began attending our laughter rounds off and on.

As a rule, at the end of each session the participants relax and share their experiences. This is a touching, moving moment when raw emotions are exposed—those from laughter *and* those from distress. Some people even break down into tears as a release of their pent-up stress. We uncover a lot of loneliness, depression, and despair amongst the everyday people who attend, and send them home with a lighter heart. These grounding sessions after the great emotional release from hearty laughter helps the group to touch and heal their souls, and is perhaps the foremost reason why I have found such meaning in spreading laughter.

The rich lady I referred to was a bit scornful and dismissive at the start, but somewhere down the road, something struck a chord in her. I noticed a mellowing in her attitude as time went by. She actively joined in our discussions, until one day she asked to be trained as a laughter leader. I jokingly jabbed, "Is it to do parties?" to which she didn't answer, but her moist, beseeching eyes said it all.

In retrospect, I can conclude that this lady had it all—money, looks, youth—but still needed to identify with humanity, to discover something more meaningful in herself and her world. Time has gone by, and she's now a respected laughter leader with a robust following. She's found a meaning in what she's doing and has thrown herself with passion into bettering peoples' lives in this way.

I think all of us have an inner thirst to find meaning in our lives. I feel that people who shy away from this natural urge are spiritually bankrupt. They haven't experienced the most fascinating attraction that life offers.

The bankrupt people you're referring to aren't exactly dying of deprivation. Quite the reverse—they'll keep toasting life's attractions and dump you in the loony bin.

Sure, they'll be gorging on possessions, lording their power over others, and feel over the moon with what they've achieved. The point here is that power and possessions offer pleasures that light up the brain only temporarily and to a shallow depth. This is a poor serving of life. The greater, stronger, and more lasting joy and ecstasy comes from discovering your purpose and meaning in life.

True taste and zestful living is in enjoying the whole smorgasbord, the big, brimming buffet of life's delights. Not just the most popular, fatty chow.

Aha! And you're the high priest who knows what people enjoy most.

You're the high priest, Mr. D—not me. I'm just a small-time nobody who's found a perennial treasure trove. I've come to you for its valuation and validation. So I can share it with the world and urge others to feel firsthand the unique joys of finding purpose in life.

Purpose, schmurpose. Pie in the sky, gone and good-bye. Most people don't miss a thing by failing to pursue a purpose.

Those who live without a *purpose* are drifting, floundering, and drowning themselves in hedonistic activities. Without a purpose, their lives are empty so they flout and flay, and indeed turn to hatred for solace. To paraphrase Robert Byrne, since they don't stand for something, they'll fall for anything.

> *"When you are inspired by some great purpose, some extraordinary project, all your thoughts break their bonds; your mind transcends limitations, your consciousness expands in every direction, and you find yourself in a new, great, and wonderful world. Dormant forces, faculties, and talents become alive, and you discover yourself to be a greater person by far than you ever dreamed yourself to be."*
>
> —Patanjali

Don't talk in riddles! How do you specifically define this purpose, or meaning of life, that has captivated you?

A sense of meaning is a sense of relevance to the world, a role in God's creation. If in some way you're helping others or nature or God in His grand design, then you feel a great sense of fellowship and kinship with God, a feeling of belonging to a higher purpose bigger than your own self.

And what is this higher purpose?

The purpose is higher because it involves rising above our petty, selfish concerns. Each one of us is unique, so I guess everybody has a different interpretation of life, different skills and synergies, different goals. We can find purpose in little things or big things, but it leads us to higher satisfaction.

I'm talking about the purpose of the purpose. Be specific! Give examples. Pinpoint your own purpose.

One man's purpose may sound foolish to another, but that's not important. The important thing is to have a purpose to hold sway over you.

You're testing my patience! Will you come up with an example?

Okay, let's take a good and popular example. Have you ever heard of the starfish story?

No, but I'm all ears.

There's this young kid on a seashore littered with beached starfish, and he's picking them up and throwing them far into the sea one by one. Then an old man walks by and asks the kid what he's up to.

The kid explains that the waves have taken the starfish too far into the sand and they're unable to make it back to the water. Left on their own, they would dry up and die, so he's flinging some back. The old man then says that there are millions and millions of such beached starfish, so "what difference is it going to make?"

Then the kid picks up another starfish and says, "It sure makes a difference to this one!" and he flings the little creature far into the ocean.

Interesting story, but what's the meaning?

The meaning *is* the meaning. The kid out of compassion did what he could for the starfish. He found meaning in doing what he was doing. And so it is with all of us. If we can find some purpose to our life, or meaning to it, then our lives are so much richer and more fulfilling.

So what you humans want is to throw starfish back into the sea?

In a manner of speaking, yes! To give or get respect for life. A popular route to finding your life purpose is to express yourself through your creativity, such as artists, poets, and inventors do. Everyday people, too, can immerse themselves into some hobby or project that captivates them. This is an avenue of expression, an outlet of creativity. You may or may not become highly proficient in your chosen field, but if others appreciate and accept you, then this will yield a purpose to hold sway over you, a reason to live for.

Most people, however, are captivated with the idea of *making a difference*. There are myriads of meanings and methods of doing this. But insofar as your purpose is to make a positive difference to lives and the world around you, then you're on the right track.

What on earth do you see in all this? Is it about popularity and recognition, or is it about proclivity beyond the grave?

> *"He who has a why to live for can bear with almost any how."*
> —Nietzsche

What we get is a unique, distilled fulfillment. To an extent you're right: it's a cry for significance and to become a hero. But there's more to it.

When we've found a purpose to our lives, we discover a great inner energy that turns the notion of everyday tepid happiness into lasting rapture, a joy that transcends all pleasures, a connectedness to the universe.

And this is your personal ethical philosophy?

So it is. The young kid on the beach didn't read philosophy or go to school, but he found joy and fulfillment in rescuing stranded starfish. The kid's heart prodded him to do his crude math to figure out what he most liked. So it was, too, with the wealthy lady who discovered her meaning through spreading laughter.

The ultimate life purpose could generally be the same for many of us, or vary in theme or color. A common, good, and noble intention is to make the world a better place, or to make others happy or to heal or to help—each to his or her individual taste and preference.

Helping an old and infirm person to cross the road is as rewarding and meaningful as donating money to the needy. You don't have to be financially rich to heal or help others. All you need is good-heartedness. The more you focus your energy to reach out to others—give them a leg up—the more meaningful your life becomes and the more you enrich your heart.

How you express your calling is an individual journey too. The kid did it with starfish. The janitor in my office building donates his time to deliver groceries to the physically challenged. I read of a reformed drug addict who visits the cancer ward of the local hospital to tell stories to young children. A young man I know, in his early twenties, has a huge collection of jokes, which he prints onto little slips of paper and gives away to people on the subway. Each one of us is equipped with our own unique paintbrush to color the world as we wish.

> *"Life is a big canvas. Throw all the paint on it you can."*
>
> —Danny Kaye

All this mumbo jumbo is meaningless and masochistic! Why can't you just be content to hunt and hoard and be merry the way your maker intended? It's a perfectly good life without all this fuss about meaning.

Oh sure, life will go on, but aren't we humans also programmed to improve the quality of our lives? Without purpose, there is no motivation. Without motivation, there is no achievement. Without achievement, there is no joy to experience. And believe me, sir, there is no joy deeper than that which comes from experiencing true meaning, the end of purpose.

We as humans are at our best and happiest when we are creative. Not after the accomplishment but in the act of accomplishing. And accomplishment cannot be had without a purpose. So a lack of meaning brings despair and desperation, an empty life with one's vast talent pools left untapped.

Man's true measure of success is not what he gains from achieving but what he becomes through it. This great joy, a total fulfillment, is possible only when man has a purpose, a meaning. This is what gives life its ultimate worth.

Enough! I'm disgusted with your babbling on and on. You humans are animal beings, here on earth because of the biological mutation of certain living organisms. You can live a perfectly normal and complete life by enjoying all the fruit that life offers. You don't have to think that you're part of some greater plan. But you're never satisfied and seek more and more and more. If this isn't your archaic hunter-gatherer instinct, then what is?

You're right, it *is* about more and more and more, but this more and more and more is an ongoing search for a deeper and deeper joy. This is possible only by developing character and increasing our knowledge of ourselves, because pursuing these goals enriches our lives. It produces the side effects of joy like nothing else. The search for meaning is worthwhile for its own sake, not because it fulfills any mystic, unknowable purpose. It is the one search that gives bountiful rewards in opening up the taps of our own hidden inner energies so that we can enjoy our true potential.

I understand now where Gandhi got his inner strength and drive. It stemmed from a very strong sense of meaning, as an end to his focused purpose—a purpose that changed the face of the world.

Thanks a ton, Mr. D, for asking the questions that prompted and clarified my thinking. Your contrarian view forced me to examine myself better. The words I found to respond to your queries helped me build on my own beliefs. At last, I'm quite clear about purpose as the route and meaning as the ultimate experience. This is where my laughter activity is leading me to.

You talked more than I did. You're making a habit of it. I have no more questions about your childish, immature notions.

Why do you say I'm childish? I feel very mature with the meaning I've found attached to the giving I do in spreading laughter.

I will grant that you feel some satisfaction in the pursuit of your purpose, but your attempts to explain it are juvenile at best.

Maybe that's so, and I welcome a deeper insight from you. In the meantime, it doesn't matter how lofty your purpose or how humble your actual achievements toward this purpose. What matters is that you become energized the moment you begin chipping away toward it. This is true meaning and true joy as I know.

I've been meaning to say it earlier, but this chitchat is meaningless, and you're a mean so-and-so to have started it!

Whatever you say, I mean well.

As a human, you're different from the average, or the mean.

Too many meanings! What matters is the true meaning of meaning.

> *"The least of things with a meaning is worth more in life than the greatest of things without it."*
> —Carl Gustav Jung

CHAPTER 5

TO THE DEVIL HIS DUE

 It's a strange conversation that we've had. You've given a long sermon on giving and meaning. Am I supposed to applaud from the audience?

 Did I sound like that? C'mon, Mr. D—you posed so many questions.

 Only the ones you asked me to. I certainly didn't give my own standpoint on the broader picture of your concerns. I responded as you asked, with a contrarian, opposing view.

 And so you did. What did we miss?

 You talked at first about your feelings from spreading laughter, then the joys of giving and in finding meaning. In reacting to your questions, only now do I have the general drift of your queries, the broad background of your original reason in seeking me out.

 I came to you for a cross-questioning of my conclusions. For opinions that run counter to mine.

 Opinions? I haven't given you a single independent opinion. You asked for opposing views, and that's what you got.

I approached you as a counterweight to my own reasoning. Where did I go wrong?

You obviously think of me as being totally adverse, perverse, and converse, the reverse of all that is right and reasonable.

I guess so.

Ha-ha! How naive you are! We'll find out how right and reasonable I can be in a while.

You mean there's another side to you?

All in good time. In the meantime, I rather like you, despite your high-hat, holier-than-thou views. As I understand, you wanted me to question your motives—what you stand for—and reconcile this with your prickly, petulant persona.

Yes, and to validate or invalidate me and my feelings.

So far, I have followed your brief to the letter. You sought me out for a cross-examination, an interrogation of your beliefs—didn't you?

So I did.

I dutifully delivered on your request much as a lawyer does—a lawyer who can be hired to argue either side of a case, both as a plaintiff or for the defense.

And so you did, too.

In the actual case, most of what I have said does not represent my independent or complete opinion. You predisposed me and cornered me to act the inquisitor, the cross-examiner. That's not my real nature. There's more to me than simply providing a counter, converse, or contrary stance to your convictions. Other than perform a questioning, I have a lot to say on my own that's relevant to dispel your doubts.

Like what?

You'll be surprised at my knowledge on the issues that irk you. I have an insight deeper than your own superficial understanding of yourself and your world.

I welcome your perspective. You live out there in the netherworld and know more about it than I do. I'm delighted with our talk.

For starters, just for now, you must shed any preconceived fear of me, or a condemnation that I am evil. You have asked me to allay your fears, to clear your doubts. So think of me as pure knowledge.

I get the feeling that in some way you'll dissipate my dilemmas. For a start, don't you agree with my discovery of the gush from giving, the power of purpose?

As a categorical answer, I can broadly endorse your findings, but with some qualifications. I think that as we talk we can find some common ground to address your concerns.

My concerns are about the inner conflict I carry within myself. I'm violently selfish one moment, and passionately selfless the next. As you've seen, I'm bewitched with the giving that I do, and yet I'm so very impatient and intolerant of the world. I wonder who and what I am, where and how I'm going. Is this the right way? Where does it lead?

It really helped to open my heart out to you, because as I spoke I could both define and refine my feelings. It's a great relief to know that you at least partly agree with me.

I'll grant that you humans need to find a faith to lean on, and a purpose and meaning to your lives. But I maintain that your religions color and shape this urge in you to put you onto their chosen track.

How does it matter which way religion points? The point is that you find a great euphoria, an inner warmth, a sharing and connecting from giving and meaning.

Your religion has planted your notions of spirituality and caring and sharing in your heart. You cannot escape its pervasive influence.

I suppose so. Religious faith is the backbone of our social system and morality. It's what are laws our based on. Our courts have us swear the truth on our holy books.

All that you prize, the inner warmth, the euphoria of spiritual connection— is this in deference to a religious upbringing?

Maybe. I can't say for sure. But how does it matter?

It matters a great deal, as we'll see.

Let's agree that you're born with a great urge to find meaning in your life. That urge needs feasible answers to the questions that haunt you: "Who and what is man? Who and what is God? What is life and death?"

> *"For out of fear and need each religion is born, creeping into existence on the byways of reason."*
> —Friedrich Nietzsche

Religion pounces on these mysteries with ready, packaged answers in the form of God, to whom they claim a direct line. Religions portray God as the overlord who offers reward and redemption for His followers, death and damnation for the dissenters. And so they tout a judgment day, a heaven and hell. The time-tested carrot-stick theory is used to hold religion together, presented as doctrines, scriptures, and commandments.

Why do religions come across as so serious, strong, and statutory?

All religions have a sociopolitical agenda and need faith and a following as the fuel for their survival.

It's fascinating, the way you describe religion. But really, religion serves to bind people together into moral and social groups, and I can't understand why we need to question it.

Popular religions are inconsistent and incongruent in their teachings, and the subject of violent disagreements. They compete with each other as holding the best direct connection to reach God.

All religions point to God, but you're right—different religions have divergent ways to reach God.

The divergent ways have similar routes: hymns and mantras, scriptures, chapters, and verses. All to be copiously rote chanted. One of your recent popular authors touched upon a raw nerve when he mooted that the greatest story ever told could well be the greatest story ever sold.

Your religions are mammoth, multinational industries that cater to your need to appease guilt, to seek forgiveness, to invoke the odds, to hand over wish lists, to right the wrongs, to wrong the rights. They satisfy your craving for a perennially sympathetic sounding board to state your frustrations. Religious prayer panders to every flight of fancy.

In religion you have a great convenience store that fills a varied shopping list of your needs. To polish your self-esteem, to satisfy your curiosity, to find answers to the unknown, and to provide the ready routes for your need to find purpose and meaning in life. See how smug and satisfied you feel after you've visited your temples or churches or mosques—your shopping done.

> *"Most sermons sound to me like commercials—but I can't make out whether God is the Sponsor or the Product."*
>
> —Mignon McLaughlin

You can't smear religion like this. I think religion is to be credited with the development of the human race.

Sure. I don't deny this. My point is that religion hijacks the urge for connectedness, purpose, and meaning as it wells up in you. It claims to hold a monopoly on God and all things mysterious.

But all religions point to God. Surely it's the same God.

For sure! But the bare truth is that **religion is not the only route to God,** even though religion has a lot to do with God, because religions compete with each other to sell God, or their interpretation of God.

I suppose that's true.

Your psyche, your ethos, thinks that God is religion and religion is God, that the two are the same thing. Here's where I differ. In your mind's eye, you associate God with human images or figures, or stories and notions that your religion feeds you with.

You're right to some extent. I do have this imagery whenever I think of God— I recall a human form and certain gospels and hymns. It seems to me that you're not really a fan of religion. Don't you believe in God?

I have a different relationship with God than you humans. To answer your question directly—yes, I believe there's a God. But he doesn't live in your religions, which is a confusion craftily created by your clerics.

You mean God and religion are not the same thing?

> *"Religion … is the opium of the people."*
> —Karl Marx

Absolutely not! This is why I must bring religion into the reckoning, to know more about the source of your urge for giving and meaning.

This is getting technical.

God is your destination, whatever you deem Him to be. Different religions have different interpretations of God, and are alternative routes to the God they tout.

Let's say you have a common cold, one of God's free favors to the frivolous. Your grandma has her own recipe to understand and treat it, your family doctor wants to stuff you with pills, your spouse suggests megadoses of vitamin C, and your Asian friend recommends an herbal remedy.

These are different answers to the same problem. That's the way different religions have diverse answers to cure you of your dilemma on who or what is God.

I'm beginning to see the distinction between God and religion, but most people won't. The moment they think of God, they'll picture Him and remember the religious gospels, as I do.

God is your creator, and his signature masterpiece is the emotion of love and conscience that he's bestowed in your hearts. From infancy, love is the food of the soul, and children are instinctively loving, giving, and helpful. You spoke about the great joy from giving and an even greater joy felt by lending a purpose and meaning to your lives. These joys spring from the natural way God created you and have nothing to do with religion.

Have a look at the Ten Commandments. Do they talk about religion or God?

Both. They're actually some primitive religious rules.

The "rules," as you say, claim their authority from God, as being of divine origin. How does that sit with your sense of true or false?

The edicts, or commandments, were relevant for their times. Mankind needed some laws to relate to, otherwise there'd be chaos.

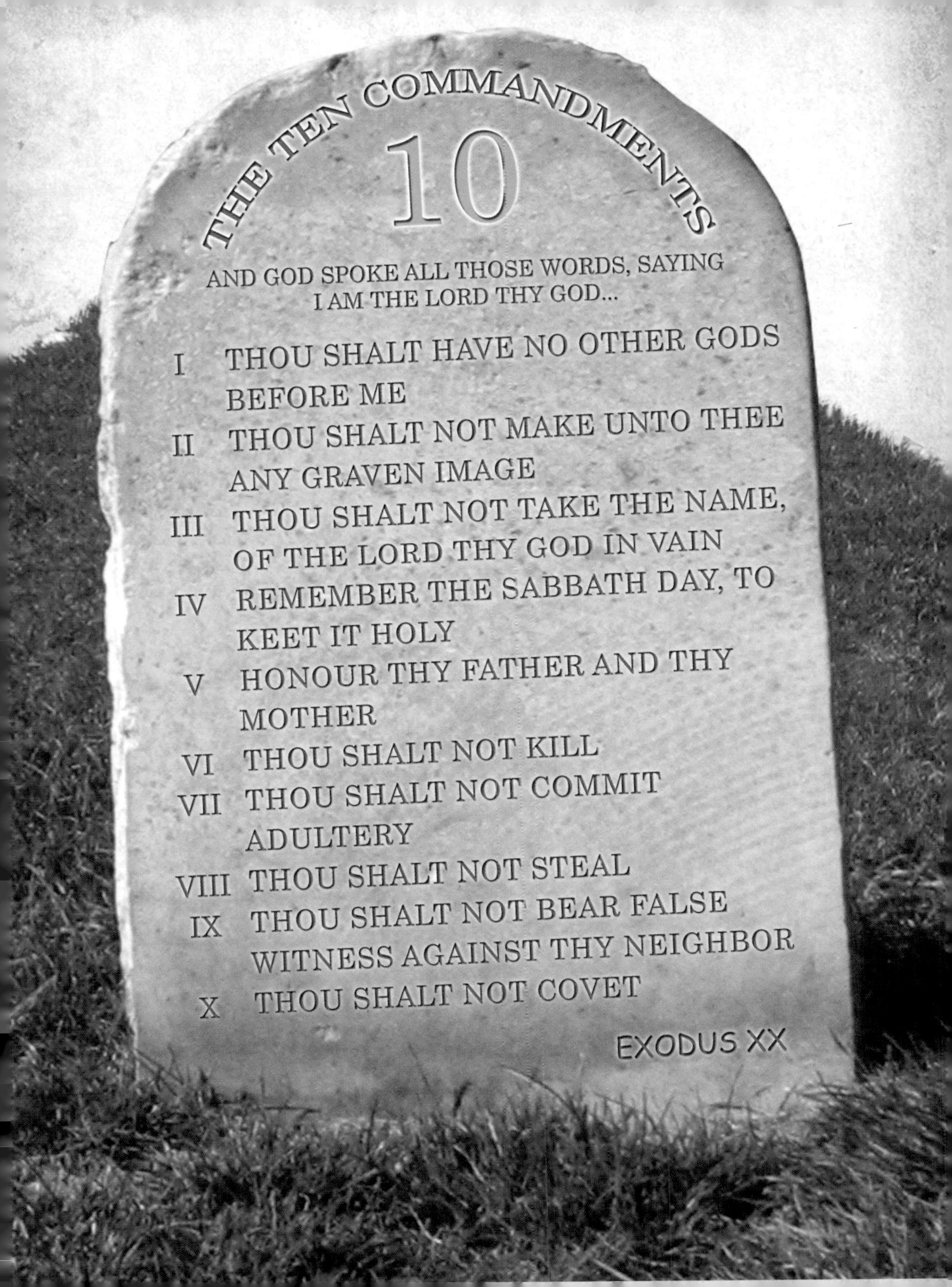
THE TEN COMMANDMENTS
10
AND GOD SPOKE ALL THOSE WORDS, SAYING
I AM THE LORD THY GOD...
I THOU SHALT HAVE NO OTHER GODS BEFORE ME
II THOU SHALT NOT MAKE UNTO THEE ANY GRAVEN IMAGE
III THOU SHALT NOT TAKE THE NAME, OF THE LORD THY GOD IN VAIN
IV REMEMBER THE SABBATH DAY, TO KEET IT HOLY
V HONOUR THY FATHER AND THY MOTHER
VI THOU SHALT NOT KILL
VII THOU SHALT NOT COMMIT ADULTERY
VIII THOU SHALT NOT STEAL
IX THOU SHALT NOT BEAR FALSE WITNESS AGAINST THY NEIGHBOR
X THOU SHALT NOT COVET
EXODUS XX

Mankind needed or mankind created these laws?

Both. Man created these laws because they were needed.

And that is religion: primitive principles and proclamations, the origin of law. Where the moral police cannot enforce their laws in present-day life, they tout offences as sins, punishable in the afterlife through a sentence to be read on "judgment day" and untold pain and suffering guaranteed in "hell." Your social systems have used religion to hijack your innocence, to plant their version of God in you.

> *"The greatest tragedy in mankind's entire history may be the hijacking of morality by religion."*
>
> - Arthur C. Clarke

Hijack? Come on, Mr. D, this is not a conspiracy with an ulterior motive. It's just an observation on how our society treats God and religion as the same thing.

I never cease to be amused and apprehensive when I witness your religious preachers, priests, and televangelists do their spirited gig in front of gaping geeks. Each tries to out-shout the other with ardent animation. All this while, a good part of your holy men's lives is the stuff of scandals—the full gamut of greed, sex, power, and perversions.

How can you be Godly without being religious?

Go back to your starfish lad. He exercised compassion in rescuing the stranded creatures. The association of working for and with God gave him a sense of meaning. Think of the poor old ladies who volunteer to work in soup kitchens, or the doctors at Médecins Sans Frontières who work for free in the most disease-stricken areas of the planet. Or countless social workers who give up lucrative careers to serve the needy.

Here you find everyday people doing meaningful, Godly things. They show you how to be Godly without being religious, whilst the world remains full of religious bloodsuckers who are anything but Godly.

You have your religious thieves and cheats, power-hungry and unscrupulous politicians, corporate ladder-climbers. Religious tyrants and bullies abound in every walk of life. Social parasites who abuse, defile, and damage nature's bountiful blessings with wild, wanton waste. Those who dupe and deceive for personal gain. Very much part of this list are your pastors, preachers, and priests who make a living by touting religion but are far from Godly in their private lives.

What you say rings true, but you can't change people's beliefs. Whatever you say, people will continue to link religion with God. All things considered, religion's a very important part of our lives that helps us develop into good, civic-minded, and moral persons. Why should God want us to stay away from religion?

God wants you to live each moment of your lives through free choice. Whether this includes religion is also your choice, because religion merely crowds the road. When you can make a direct connection with God, then why go through intermediaries who claim the best route?

What choice do we have? After all, almost all of us are already born into one or another religion and grow up under its influence.

That's unfortunate, but true. Religion does help you discover some element of morality. Yet, to find your true meaning and your true self, you need to seek your own direct relationship to God, to look beyond the veil of religion.

My religion has helped me become a good person. Try as I might, I can't agree with your radical view.

Religion is a distraction from God. If it helps to make you a good person, then look beyond religion to become an even better person.

Religion is too hardwired into my system. I instinctively hum my mantras and hymns when my mind is idling. Your view is too strong to digest.

It's a shame that your inferior, inflexible personality can't digest the truth.

I respect your opinion about religion, but how is this relevant to my original concerns about the value of *giving*, of finding *purpose* and *meaning*?

Your understanding is at best crude and childish, and focuses on the wrong stimuli for your search for meaning. Your giving, purpose, and meaning will never be perfectly pure and powerful so long as they're motivated by and connected to your religion, which is man-made and perforce inferior to what is God-made. And that is the voice of your heart, your conscience.

Hmm. That's interesting. Do carry on.

Religion is a crude and antiquated method to help you grow beyond your animal urges. Your starfish lad didn't need a priest to do the right thing: the giving thing, the meaningful and Godly thing. Your Nazi camp survivors who gave their paltry rations to the sick and dying may or may not have been religious, but were certainly Godly. Their compassion was dictated by their conscience, which alone offered the highest meaning to their lives.

I'm aware that we're all born with an inner conscience. Can you define it more completely?

Conscience is your natural protector and policeman to the love that is inherent to your inner nature. You're all born with a conscience that differentiates between good and evil better than the mind. It's an inborn instinct, untainted by the adult teaching of religion or social norms that you're subjected to. The voice of conscience sometimes tells you to behave in strange ways—to reject profit and pleasure for pain and discomfort. Conscience obliges you to do good deeds and shun evil.

You've described my feelings exactly. I'm driven more by conscience rather than religion.

> *"Religion is the masterpiece of the art of animal training, for it trains people as to how they shall think."*
>
> —Arthur Schopenhauer

Religions work through a reward-punishment, heaven-hell system—a good animal taming routine, but antiquated. Conscience works through free will and is a natural law of the universe. It is like sunshine, rain, gravity, day and night, and is indestructible. Unlike your man-made religions.

Conscience elevates you to react to protect your love, to morally do the right thing.

Don't religions teach you to love and care, the same as conscience? Surely both are quite similar as guidance systems?

Conscience and religion often dictate the same code of ethics, but are sometimes at odds with each other. You're a religious non-vegetarian and enjoy your lamb chops and kebabs, but will you slaughter the lamb without a twinge of conscience? Many religions subjugate women to slavery. How does this sit with your conscience of right and wrong? Most religions are fiercely protective of their flock and discourage defections, or active assistance to other faiths. These territorial confines don't apply to conscience, which is your innate urge to love and help one and all.

Your heart listens instinctively more to conscience rather than earthly religious programming. Your search for meaning is actually born out of conscience, but then waylaid by religion.

> *"Conscience is our magnetic compass; reason our chart."*
> —Joseph Cook

You mean we should disentangle and detach conscience from religion. View the two as independent value systems, driving forces of how to feel, think, and behave?

Precisely. Your moral values perforce originate from your religion, which traps and ensnares your urge to find meaning before your mind strays to alternative answers. You're encouraged to follow their neat, narrow, and ready road to spiritual salvation. Each religion claims to have a monopoly on God and prescribes copious reciting and chanting as the road to heaven. You're told that the ritual motions of attending holy sermons and visiting your places of worship will erase your sins.

And since your religions can't deliver on their promises in your present life, you're conveniently told to wait for these in your afterlife, or heaven.

Please, Mr. D—it's not for us to question the existence of religion. It's here to stay, at least for now. The fact remains that without religion we'd probably still be cavemen with no sense of organization and assembly. Religion has brought to our species economic, physical, mental, and even some spiritual advancement. I do agree with you that religion is an easy groove to fall into for those seeking spirituality. It should be possible to be religious without believing in religion, and to be spiritual without attaching religion to it.

Won't happen. Any wandering of the imagination is bulldozed too soon in life by your religions. You get laughed out, scorned, and persecuted if you don't conform.

You used some good superlatives in describing your feelings from giving and pursuing meaning. You felt connected, felt an inner warmth, or great gush, or ultimate experience, or spiritual upliftment. You felt these feelings without any religious compulsion or religious leanings.

I guess you're right. You can be good and reap the joys of being good without involving religion.

Your conscience is a natural universal law. You subconsciously trust your inner voice of conscience more than written laws and regulations. In a way, religion tries to overtake and overwrite your conscience, but succeeds only partly because there's an element of conscience that you can't erase, can't overwrite.

It's amazing how you've dissected religion. I wonder what you'll say about God.

Plenty. But tell me something—your religious holy books are full of different descriptions of God and his power. You'll find volumes and encyclopedias on the subject. Why ask me, the anti-God?

I don't trust the religious interpretations, and I'm too lazy to study all the tomes and treatises on God. Somehow I value your opinion and explanation more than the common ones. The way you talked about God a while ago, it was very restrained, without any rabid references. Really, Mr. D, I expected you to decry and denounce God, who you spar with.

So you've typecast me, picturized me as a fire-breathing monster?

The world sees you as evil and pictures you as such. As the anti-God, you come across as the opposite of all that is loving and giving and merciful. Isn't God your nemesis?

I'll ignore your misgivings about me. You think that God is the mightiest being, some sort of final authority, a keeper of heaven and hell. Able to perform miracles, fulfill your desires, and come to your rescue in times of need.

I suppose that's a good description, though not complete. To me, God is the most powerful being there is, a great source of wonder. He puts joy in our hearts.

Hmm, so you think of God as a being.

In a manner of speaking. But what's your own complete description of God?

Do you think any description of God can be complete?

That's my question to you. Can you describe God in a few words?

It's like asking somebody to define the meaning of the word **love** in one line. Can you do that?

I can't, but I think *you* can.

Traditionally, the word God is the name you give to whatever you can't understand and explain. Your religions have seized this mystery for their own ends and obscured the true meaning.

As a concise definition, I'll say that above all, God is the master creator of all there is. His greatest creation is love, the most powerful force that exists on the planet. Love is the grandest and primary emotion, which manifests into feelings of affection, joy, zest, and optimism. This is the core energy source of the human race to live and progress in life.

Love is what connects you, focuses your energies, motivates you, and holds humanity together. Your science and technology may one day replicate and clone physical humans, but it cannot create love in a laboratory. And since God created love, the one-liner caption for the two is identical, which is the **force that helps you bring out your best**.

God, or his love, is the conviction you hold that His power is with you. It keeps you going in the face of adversity. A short while ago, when you described your search for meaning, you mentioned the euphoria as "feeling connected, close to, and one with God."

That's a novel and interesting way to define God. But I'm surprised why you as the anti-God can describe God in such glowing terms. If God is what you say He is, then how do you describe yourself, his opponent and enemy?

First, tell me where you think God lives.

In heaven, I suppose. But we're told he's here on Earth too, in our churches, mosques, and temples. We seek him out whenever we need him, or when we pray to him.

I will put it bluntly; there is no God in your temples or churches or mosques, nor in your pictures, crosses, trinkets, and figurines, nor in your holy books and holy water. God is not something you can touch or hold but is something you feel. You go to your places of worship to remember God, to renew your faith and belief in God.

You mean the pictures and statues of Jesus, of the Buddha, the Hindu, and other Gods mean nothing?

Once again you are confusing God with religions. Jesus, the Buddha, and the Hindu Gods are perceived as the emissaries who brought Godliness to earth and are therefore worshipped. But to answer you directly, there is no God in these images and statues that you have created to focus and fixate your imagination. You do this because you need a physical being to worship, with real arms and legs. You need to give a face and form to whom or what you adore and worship. In the actual case, **God lives in your hearts and minds as a faith**, as a belief, as a credo and conviction that He is there. God is your pillar of faith and acts as your power source to exercise love and hope. In moments of great peace, calm, and joy, many of you exclaim that you're "one" with God. That means you're at peace with your inner self, with your conscience, with God.

You mean our holy books are just storybooks?

I have no wish to discredit or insult your holy books that you swear upon in your courts of law as the embodiment of God. I have already said that God and religion are not identical. Your holy books are a clever man-made tool to remind you of your faith in God, but there is no God in these stories and scriptures.

Our shops sell religious books, images, and figurines as the embodiment of God.

As reminders of God and their version of God. The God that punishes as freely as he loves and rules by infusing fear into the errant nonbelievers.

In truth, God is pure love, pure giving, pure forgiving. Fear is something he banishes with the courage and strength He provides. God doesn't want to scare you into submission; rather, He magnetizes you with His magnanimity. God helps you to discover your deepest strength. God is the Creator of all there is.

You're right. When I brood even for a minute on the miracle of creation, I can't cease to be amazed. When I dwell upon the glory of God, I sense the same warm glow in my heart that I feel in the act of giving, in finding meaning.

Your heart is where God lives: in your perception, your wonderment, your feelings, and your faith.

Your picture of God is awesome. But I'm equally curious about who you are, how you define yourself, the devil and anti-God?

I am the diametrical opposite of God. If God is love, then I am fear, anger, hatred, and suffering.

You're all these horrible things?

To understand me better, you should first know how I came to be. Did you ever wonder about who exactly created the devil, or Satan—that's me?

Never thought about it. I guess when God was creating the world, you somehow slipped through from somewhere.

God created everything, so if you're saying I slipped through the cracks somewhere, then that somewhere was also created by God.

I suppose when God was making humans, you were the defective model that sprung to life and ran away. And you somehow stole some of his powers.

Ran away where, and how? The only thing running is your imagination. If God could create the world and everything in it, surely he had the power to capture me and throw me into recycling?

What? Are you suggesting that God created you? You're the devil and stand for everything against Him—why'd He do that?

Take a guess!

Beats me. Unless it was to demonstrate his power over evil in some way.

Here's my point:

Without the anti-God, there is no God, since mankind will never be able to understand and appreciate the presence of God without a provocation.

When I, the anti-God, have put you into trouble and sickness, you rush to find God as your savior and healer.

Look around you: the only time you humans remember God is when I'm lurking around you causing hurt, harm, and hardship. You don't need God for your daily survival, or when the going's good. Only when you hit misfortune, accidents, ill health, or bereavement do you remember God.

The other time you need God is when you're trying to dispel fear and rise up with courage. Often, you remember God through prayer when there's a great calamity at the door. One way or another, God is a countermeasure and cure to all your problems. And these problems are planted there by me, the devil, or Satan. Call me what you wish.

Oh my God! You're a creation of God?

> *"It always strikes me, and it is very peculiar, that when we see the image of indescribable and unutterable desolation—of loneliness, of poverty and misery, the end of all things, or their extreme—then rises in our mind the thought of God."*
>
> —Vincent Van Gogh

Just as you are, and for a good reason. God is a faith, a belief just as I, the anti-God, am. In your physical world, both are unreal. Both are ethereal. I'm God's partner because I prove and perpetuate his existence better than anything else. You feel the need for God only as a solution to your plight from pain and misery. I am the "dote" to which God is the antidote and vice versa.

This is your persona, how you were created. You understand and appreciate the meaning of relief from suffering only when you undergo distress. Light is called light to explain the opposite of darkness, and light exists because there is darkness. I am the dark anti-God that the light of God dispels. Either way, God can exist because I coexist.

Are you a part of God?

As you are, my dear chap. God is the ultimate Creator.

Gosh! I'm too dumbfounded to think.

To cherish freedom, you need to taste fear. The fear that makes you freeze, fight, or flee, as your natural primal reaction. Unless you draw out the God within you—that's your courage—you cannot fight fear, because courage is what conquers fear.

Are you saying that God created you to do the opposite of what He does?

I bring God closer to you humans than any other force on earth. Your species is lazy, complacent, and naive. You never get around to finding your strengths unless I prod you with pain, scare you with starvation. **You need the worst to bring out your best.**

I'll put it this way: God exists for you as an end to the suffering that the anti-God puts you through. As with all mortals, you are programmed to pursue your happiness and shun any suffering and sickness, the prospect of which scares you into seeking salvation. This is how you stumble through your entire life, where you seek support and solace as an end to struggle and sorrow.

> *"If it weren't for the dark days, we wouldn't know what it is to walk in the light."*
>
> —Earl Campbell

You said that God is the force that helps us bring out our best. You mean God helps us bring out our best through his opposite, that's you—the anti-God?

I am what clarifies and defines your sensation of God. If there is no opposite of God, then you won't be able to identify and understand Him.

You said that God lives in our hearts as a faith. Is that where *you* live as well?

Yes. Just as God lives in your hearts as a belief, so do I also live in your hearts as doubt and disbelief, as the source of all your anxieties, fears, self-doubt, angers, and worries. I go where He goes. I live where He lives.

I'm getting the picture. I suppose it's easier to believe in God and His glory because there's a counter to Him. That's how it works with every concept or emotion in this world—a choice from opposites. I can marvel at the genius of God, to design this world, His creation, to be felt and recognized in this way.

THE CHEROKEE

One evening, an old Cherokee Indian told his grandson about a battle that goes on inside people. He said, "My son, the battle is between two wolves inside us all. One is Evil. It is anger, envy, jealousy, sorrow, regret, greed, arrogance, self-pity, guilt, resentment, inferiority, lies, false pride, superiority, and ego. The other is Good. It is joy, peace, love, hope, serenity, humility, kindness, benevolence, empathy, generosity, truth, compassion, and faith."

The grandson thought about it for a minute and then asked his grandfather, "Which wolf wins?"

The old Cherokee simply replied, "The one you feed."

You come to believe and feel God out of free choice because it is the only way anything is welcome in your heart: without any coaxing or compulsion. It is easy to look for God and find Him when I, the anti-God, am lurking around, staring you in the face!

Only when you're hurt do you truly appreciate the value of love. Because love is the only thing that can heal hurt. So it is with God, because you acknowledge Him as your savior only when you desperately need Him to escape from the wrath of the anti-God.

I suppose that's where you figure in this grand scheme of things?

I'm the dark part of the big array of choices you're presented. I'm all your self-doubts, fears, temptations, angers, jealousies. I live inside your hearts to put the question mark of suspicion and skepticism on every constructive thing you do. I am also your pride, your vanity and ego. When I can't influence you through your own mind and heart, I sit in the department of bad luck to draw you back into your dark self.

You're all those things?

And more. I strike with venom like a poisonous rattlesnake quite randomly. I maim, hurt, and destroy just for the heck of it. The moment you start building any sandcastles, I make sure to kick the sand right into your face. Often, I strike you blind with rage and egg you on to maltreat, maim, and murder your own kind.

You're a real monster, Mr. D. Do you enjoy doing all this?

It's all in a day's work. I do it with my eyes closed. Enjoyment does not occur to me; I just do the work I'm designed for. I am impervious to the wild cries and gasps as I snuff the breath out of my victims.

What a sadist you are! God would never create such a monster as you!

But He did, as the antithesis of himself, and for a good reason. You seek and savor God only because I'm there to sway you toward Him.

That's a roundabout and dangerous way to reach God.

Your worldly success—and spiritual success—comes to you not as a birthright, but through a painful journey of discovery. And I am the head of the pain department. Pleasure is cherished best after incurring pain, and God is valued most as an escape from the anti-God. You treasure most what you have most suffered and fought for.

I'm still confused. You drop pearls of wisdom one moment and commit death and destruction the other. How can you do what you do? You destroy all the good that God does. You undo His doing.

The Creator modeled me differently from you humans. I was made to be at ease with rage and ravage. I work with robotic efficiency to hit and hurt randomly. As a superior being to you, I can read you as an open book. When I see order, love, and purity, my response is to mar and mask it with disorder, hate, and corruption. I wasn't made to recoil from my duty.

Just as you are programmed to act as you do, so am I programmed by the Creator. I'm a part of God's plan in this world, just as you are. I was created to put you through hardships and handicaps so that you can seek and study the skills to surmount them. Before you blame me, remember that I'm the soldier here, helping you win your wars.

I'm the one who planted your own self-doubts and anxieties in you when you sought me out.

Oh my God, are you pointing me back to those feelings, the insecurity and incredulity I feel with my own self?

Precisely! Go back to your disbelief and distrust. Your suspicion and skepticism. As a child, you were trusting and playful, but I made sure that time would ravage and ransack your innocence to desensitize you. As you grew up to face the world, I lent a hand by littering your way with problems and predicaments so as to strengthen your resolve.

I'm too confused to think. Why would God make it so difficult to reach Him?

Think again. You wouldn't need God without the trigger or stimulus of problems to point you towards Him. You can blame your ignorance, indifference, or indolence, but few of you would seek God without my constant reminders. When you face adversity, you discover the great power of your own brains and your capabilities, which you exploit and exercise only because I force this action on you. God's way is really a victory over your own shortcomings.

I can understand your reasoning. I'm just a bit put out that God who loves us puts so many obstacles in our way.

Most of your worries are imagined, but you waste yourselves, dampen your spirits, and blunt your courage by worrying. Eventually, when you do endure and survive, your relief knows no bounds.

If I, Satan, am the chief instigator and engineer of your worries, then you can either blame me to eternity, or learn to live with me. One way or another, I live in your hearts and will continue to feed on your failings and frailties until you face me.

How do you face somebody without a face?

My face is your fears, anxieties, guilt, self-doubt, angers, and envy, everything that holds you back.

I'm stumped. Are you suggesting that God can be reached only through a big obstacle course? By scaling a huge mountain?

The mountain is your own fear and incredulity that you need to suppress. Your biggest obstacle is yourself.

Oh my God!

Does "Oh my God" come easier to your mind than "What the Devil"? I have a thankless job. You humans gripe, groan, and growl about the hardships and headaches you go through in life. How about my suffering when all I have to look forward to is to be squashed, stifled, and smothered?

Oh, I never looked at it from your side. You're right, Mr. D. I owe you a big apology. I've been disrespectful and scared of you.

I don't blame you! Comes with the job. God made me to face fear and loathing with ease. I can't expect you humans to come to love me the way you adore and worship God, but I can certainly do with a bit of respect and understanding.

I can't bring myself to sing your praises and love you, because you're the face of all my problems. But I certainly have a new respect for you. Given time, I could begin to look upon you with a new awareness. There's a great relief in not having to react with alarm and anxiety now, when fear, guilt, or bad luck weigh me down.

Aha! Now there's at least one human who sympathizes with me!

I have a question: Why are you so forthcoming with me? On the face of it, I'm a nobody out of nowhere coming to you with nonsense. Yet you took the time to talk to me.

I am not God's enemy, but his alter ego and antithesis. I am equally a part of God who rewards those who seek with humility and sincerity. It's a depressing department that I head and a lonely life I lead. That's why I agreed to this conversation with you. It's not right to look upon me with dread and loathing when I'm actually your best friend to point you in the right direction.

My name in your earthly dictionary is lumped with the worst of the worst. You use my name freely as some of the most detestable abuses you can hurl on anybody. I am visualized as ghastly and gruesome. Mothers routinely use my name to terrify their children into submission. Even the thought of me is revolting and horrendous. Your disciples of divinity have drawn me with horns, fangs, claws, and bulgy eyes, ready to pounce on you with a spear in my hand.

You're really not the beast you're made out to be.

But *you* are! Beastly to the core. It's your preset condition, as in "the nature of the beast," which best describes your makeup. You use me to justify and rationalize your laziness and inaction, or when you poison yourselves with anger and jealousy and hatred. In the actual case, you are the chief impediment to your higher nature, to finding yourself.

You think of me as a villain, an outside force that hurts you and blocks you. But the truth is that I live in your own hearts, as an inner force that you need to understand and subdue.

In the meantime my work is thankless, and you must have the grace to **give the devil his due**.

> *"Give the devil his due."*
> —Miguel de Cervantes Saavedra

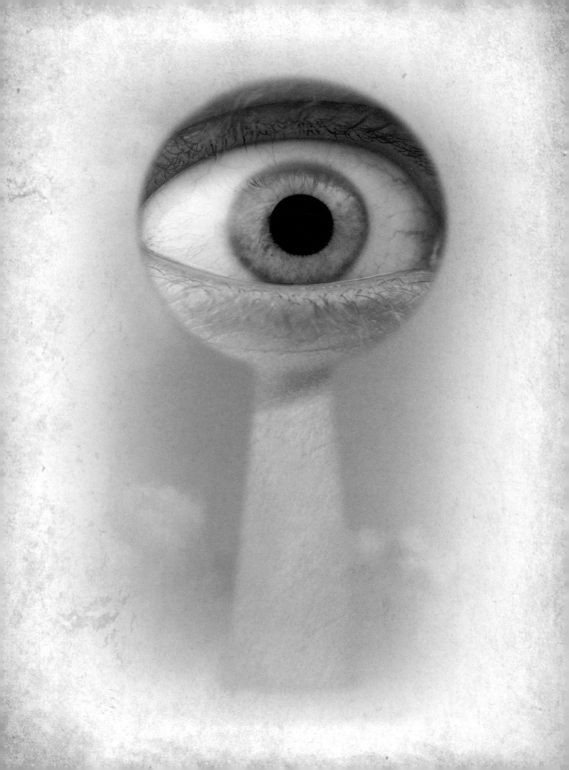

CHAPTER 6

NATURE OF THE BEAST

 You called me beastly, Mr. D—that's not fair!

 Fair or not, now I'll talk about the what, why, and how you humans tick. This is a whole new subject, so you can understand the nature of the beast that you are. You're not too different from animals, with the same physical organs and biological cycle. Tell me, where and how, as a human being, do you sit in the animal kingdom?

 We're not animals in a zoo, we're intelligent humans.

 But you're a mammal that evolved from animals.

 I don't deny this, but we've advanced far beyond our animal origins. As a percentage of body weight, the human brain is the largest amongst all living species, so our memory and intelligence can't be compared to that of animals.

 Humans and animals are both a part of God's creation. And yet you're a strange breed. You fret and fume, undergo stress, nervousness, and all sorts of agony during your lives. Other than pets, you're the only animal that becomes overweight.

 I guess you're right. Intelligence cuts both ways, like a two-edged sword. The brain's prowess is behind the achievements and development of the human race, but a fertile brain misdirected or improperly used can lead to tension and trauma.

Quite so. Animals can neither promote nor demote their condition, but for you humans, **your brain both lifts and lowers your lot**, depending on how you apply it. Your history is full of thinkers, philosophers, artists, scientists and leaders in every field, who blazed new trails for humankind. Conversely, many of you are unable to handle the pulsating energy of the brain and sink into depression and even suicide. Many of you feel crowded and confused by the brain's hyperactivity and intensity. You take refuge in extreme overindulgence, such as obesity, alcoholism, and drug addiction.

Over the ages, humans have challenged, stretched, and expanded the miraculous powers of the brain for both good and bad—for benefit and betterment on the one hand, ravage and ruin on the other.

Indeed, the brain is a smart and fast computer and also blessed with imagination.

> *"My own brain is to me the most unaccountable of machinery—always buzzing, humming, soaring, roaring, diving, and then buried in mud."*
> —Virginia Woolf

The imagination which leads your motivation, for better or for worse.

Isn't imagination also the source of romance?

You can add romance to the love of another person, to poetry, to scenic beauty—whatever. You're right, imagination fires romance, just as imagination backfires into depression and human excesses that entice you to self-destruct.

There's no compulsion to take your imagination beyond dreams.

None at all, but you're blessed with a brain, with the power to think and imagine and visualize for a reason: to help you actualize your dreams and yourselves, to realize your potential, so that your lives exceed those of mere animals. After all, any animal can graze, reproduce, and live out its days.

But God gave brains to you humans for a reason, to reach for and realize your best.

You make it seem like a big test.

Indeed, your imagination can make the slightest twist seem like a big test, or make an impossible situation seem like a breeze. And many of you are quite indifferent to using your imagination at all.

This is an option God gives to all humans, not a compulsion. Many of us are perfectly content to lead mechanical lives. Without the hassle of negotiating all the blind alleys, lurking dangers, dead ends.

If you're referring to yourself, I've already scanned your mind. You're short on intelligence and big on complacency!

Sometimes I envy other animals. It's a simple preprogrammed life with no complications.

Yes, but you humans were blessed with intelligence for a reason. Growing old any animal is capable of. Growing up is the prerogative of human beings. Each of you is different, with uniquely individual capabilities and circumstances. You're the only animals capable of using your mind, heart, and spirit to realize a better and more fulfilling life.

So life is a big struggle. Like an exam?

Like a playing field. You're supposed to enjoy life, not suffer it. Playing the game is compulsory, and for play. Winning the game is an option. But most of you lead lives of quiet desperation without even playing, without tapping your potential.

I'm sure not all of us are like that. Some of us do reach for the stars.

Indeed, a handful of you are self-starters with zeal and zest, joyfully relishing each day of life even as you win some, lose some. But the majority of you are full of anger, vengeance, complaints, and cynicism all through your lives. You remain riveted to your intolerance, self-doubt, and worries. You remain unfulfilled. You feel misunderstood and empty, cynical and intolerant. And by the way, do we know somebody who is undergoing similar feelings?

Gee—are you talking about me?

Who else? You're not only short on sharpness but short on memory too.

Oops. I suppose I *am* guilty. I guess it's because I'm sometimes dulled by the demands of day-to-day life. I try my best to occupy myself with meaningful activities, but I'm still cynical and skeptical of others and myself. That's why I sought you.

I wonder why life has so many problems. Surely there's an easy way around.

You need a guarantee of success even before you try? Remember the board games, puzzles, and other games you played as a kid? The easier they were, the quicker you got bored with them. What captivated you were the games where success was dependent on the skills you developed. These are the games that you continue to enjoy well into adulthood, where the challenge and uncertainty tickle your interest and nudge you to improve and perfect your skills.

You grow out of your dolls and toy soldiers very fast, but retain your interest in crossword puzzles, card or board games, and sports that summon and stimulate your aptitude, intelligence, and prowess. A hobby such as playing a musical instrument, flying a kite, gardening, or sewing serves to absorb your attention and energy well into your old age.

In your work life and careers, you enjoy the jobs that offer you responsibility that taxes your training and your mental fortitude. A trained surgeon would be bored to work as a receptionist in a hospital, just as a financial analyst wouldn't hold on to a bus driver's job. For a career to be rewarding, it needs to exercise your acquired skills and coax your creativity, just as games and sports do.

Now that you put it this way, I guess you're right. But life is no game. If you lose, you end up with despair. I'm no gambler, Mr. D—and not with these stakes.

Sure, life is no game. But life is play all the same. You're supposed to enjoy it. Develop and push your skills to the limit. Cherish every moment.

How can you enjoy life if others are bad players but still winning? Or just lucky and winning? Or cheating and still winning?

This happens in just about every game or sport. This is how it is with the challenges of real life. What's new? It's what makes the game interesting, to prevail against all the nuances and odds.

Granted. But look—you enter a game or sport knowing that's what it is. You're free to walk out, or just give up, and you can start another one at any time. That's what makes games easy, but with life it's different.

You get lots of chances in life too. You fail, you try again. You fail again, you try yet again. If one type of game doesn't suit you, try another. If one approach fails, try the next.

What if you've tried and tried for years but aren't getting anywhere?

This should make your game, or the adventure of life, even more interesting. If you keep your buoyancy and spirit alive, if you learn from your failures and develop new skills, then you will become a better player. In the actual case, most of you don't even try. You give up too early and become bitter with being beaten. You're born with a much bigger brain than other animals but actually use no more than 5 percent of its capacity or capability. It's a shame that **most people put their potential to little use**.

What a tragedy that, for want of reaching out, most of you give up too early, too easily, and then sleepwalk through life with the song still inside you.

If the ultimate victory's mine, a million will do fine for me.

Your victory is over yourself and your earthly shortcomings. You get so bogged down with your failures that you lose touch with your abilities and all the gifts of talent that you're born with. You stop trying to realize your dreams.

You make it sound so easy. Most of us tax ourselves dry to meet the challenges of life. We're forced to live with both social limitations and obligations even as we reach for more. Often the world is cruel and doesn't reward these efforts. How can we not be bitter, resentful, and depressed? Success doesn't come easily to all of us.

It's how you define your success. You put preconditions to even your dreams of it. If only I had the looks of so and so, if only I won the lottery, if only I wasn't so fat, if only my mother-in-law didn't exist, or that show-off neighbor suffered a big calamity. If only I had that big house and a Mercedes, if only I had a million bucks…

Not all of us live in a fantasy world. We're practical, down-to-earth people living lawful lives. We know that unrealistic dreams are just that—dreams.

I'm talking about other human frailties that cloud your vision. For most of you, life is chasing an imaginary rainbow. You think that life will be better after you've made some money, when you get a promotion, or after you've found a soul mate. Then you're frustrated that your mate constrains your activities and wistfully think of your freedom. You dream of how your life will be complete when you move into a bigger house, take a vacation, or retire.

But these are real challenges. The demands of day-to-day life are enough to exhaust the best of us! We've got to wait for these demands to taper off first.

Oh, so you're waiting to attend to some unfinished business before you enjoy your life or pursue your dream? Waiting for what? Is it to finish school or to go back to school? Until you lose ten pounds or gain ten pounds? Until you have kids or until your kids leave the house? Until you get married, until you get divorced, until your car and home are paid off, until your bonus check is cashed? Or until the weekend or next weekend or spring or the holidays? Until you start work or until you retire from work? Until you die or until you're reborn?

> *"For a long time it had seemed to me that life was about to begin—real life. But there was always some obstacle in the way, something to be got through first, some unfinished business, time still to be served, or a debt to be paid. Then life would begin. At last it dawned on me that these obstacles were my life."*
>
> —Alfred D'Souza

These are all very real concerns…

Sure. So is sloth.

What's sloth?

Sloth is an attitude of dullness and indifference, which makes the task seem bigger than it is. Your scriptures have labeled sloth as one of the traditional seven root sins, along with pride, covetousness, lust, anger, envy, and gluttony.

> *"That destructive siren, sloth, is ever to be avoided."*
> —Horace

That's interesting, but I thought that you despised all scriptures.

I'm skeptical of religions, not all their teachings. I maintain that **all humans are slothful to some extent.**

That's not very flattering, but I suppose it's true. A man needs his rest and recreation.

I don't deny this, but when you overdo recreation to douse your dreams, then it's your sluggishness and sloth. Surely you can do better!

I suppose so. As humans, we can surely do better than animals.

As surely as the sun rises each morning and sets each eve, each of you humans will have your share of good and bad fortune, ups and downs, challenges, difficulties, distresses, and despairs. It's not about lamenting the cards you were dealt, but making and playing the best of the actual deal.

That's well said, but too philosophical and esoteric. Your heavenly wisdom won't appeal to everybody.

You're the one who asked me to talk. Then why do you become so sensitive when we discuss your failings?

Oh, never mind. I was just making a comment.

I have another observation, about the timing, method, and manner of your reactions when you do rise up from your slack and sloth.

Aha! So we do rise up from it.

Go back to the times when you've shed your sloth, when you've acted quickly and decisively. Can you recall those moments from your experiences?

That's easy. Once I saw a street thug pushing over a defenseless old lady to steal her handbag. I don't know what came over me. I chased, accosted, and practically threw myself at the mugger to recover the bag, and…

Did you show off your bruises for months after the ordeal?

Oh c'mon, Mr. D, why deny me my moment of glory?

Can you pick on something less dramatic?

I remember in school they had mock tests for the Board Final Exams, and I badly failed my physics and math. So I made a promise to myself and took up private coaching with a vengeance.

And did you come through?

With flying colors. I got an A in both subjects.

Think of everyday events.

Oh. The toothache got me to the dentist in double quick time.

Another reaction to extremes. Can you think of humdrum events that made you get up and go? Without further ado?

When we got snowed under, I rushed to get a shovel. And when the car battery died, I remember I walked a mile to get a charger.

Look for a pattern to your actions. Only when faced with a crisis did you rush to act.

I suppose that's true, but why would somebody in his right mind act without any crisis?

And that, my dear, explains your psyche—you act only to save your life, to avert a contingency. You set aside your inhibitions, laziness, or inertia when confronted with a crisis of some sort. You work best when pushed, when it is a compulsion. Remember how you seek and recognize God only when compelled through the anti-God?

I recall that talk.

And this logic, my dear chap, applies equally to your actions or reactions, your work and the application of your energies, because you need the worst to bring out your best.

That's taking it to the extreme. It's not always so.

Believe in Yourself

If you think you're beaten ....you already are
If you think you dare not ....you don't
If you'd like to win but think you can't ......you won't
If you think you'll lose.........................you surely will

For out in the world we find

SUCCESS BEGINS WITH A FELLOW'S WILL

Its all in a state of mind
Life's battles dont always go to the stronger or faster man,

But sooner or later,

The man who wins is the one who *THINKS* he can!

But mostly so. The truth is that your best emerges only when you're pushed to the limit by a trigger—force of circumstances, competition. Or the emotional stimulus from a loved or hated one.

As a parent, if the safety of your child is threatened, then your tame kitten heart becomes that of a tiger. You defend your loved one with valor. What gives you the courage?

A threat to what we love most.

When what you most cherish is at stake, you fight courageously. When your principles and faith are challenged, it is a blow to your self-esteem and you are blinded with rage.

You could say that's also the nature of the beast!

Ha-ha! I like people who can laugh at themselves! In a crisis, or a confrontation or challenge, you rise up with your best as an automatic reaction. What if there is no outside trigger to get you going? Will you yet put in your best as a voluntary effort out of conscious choice?

That's a difficult one. If the motive is strong enough, most of us will go for it.

Tell me something, did you not fail many times in life, a relationship, a job, a skill, reaching out for your beliefs?

Sure, failure is part of life. You've got to learn to accept it.

Did you find it easy to face the very people you intended to impress? Were you not discouraged?

I was. In fact, many a time I simply gave up.

You may have given up without a qualm. As most of you do, on your aspirations, your principles, your dreams, relationships, your play, your work.

Are you making fun of us humans?

Not at all. I'm simply pointing out your follies and foibles. Are you driving your life, or is your life driving you?

You get rebuffed and rejected when you fail. That's a big turnoff to trying. It's stupid to risk people scoffing at you and thinking you're a fool.

Failure means social ridicule and therefore creates fear in your heart. With this fear of others' indifference to your extra enthusiasm, you become self-conscious and skeptical of your own self.

Where is all this leading to?

To further define the nature of the beast. When it comes to raising a finger to pursue your dreams, the fear of failure haunts you. Fear is a constraining force and negative energy. It practically guarantees defeat. When you are in the fear mode, the comfort of your current situation cloaks you. Sloth takes over. When you do take little steps forward, it is not with conviction, and you give up easily, often blaming the world. With no zeal to surge forward, you find it safer and easier to become skeptical about life's possibilities.

Face it, only a very small handful of you are not emotionally ground to failure. You fear fear itself.

You can't simply pull a switch and turn fear off. What are you trying to say?

Being defeated is often a temporary condition. Giving up is what makes it permanent. And yet there are ways to "pull the switch" and replace fear with courage, but more on that later.

Your famous inventors didn't succeed because of luck, but because they were able to handle disappointment and failure. They were able to silence their internal self-doubt and skepticism because they believed in themselves. Your best leaders, in politics, business, or everyday life plug on at their work in spite of repeated failures. Rowland Macy faced multiple failures with his retailing attempts and survived bankruptcy before he finally succeeded with the world's largest department store that bears his name.

You've got to admire such great people. No wonder they were great.

Life is an attitude. You win some, you lose some. The enjoyment is the race. Over the long haul, the winners are those who learn to handle their misfortunes, who improve their mental ability to handle failure. Your ability to bounce back is what counts. The research study findings of your famous Martin Seligman prove that adaptable, resilient people are happier.

Not all of us see the light, or the luck. Not everybody has the get-up-and-go that you're talking of.

When fear overpowers you, your dreams are relegated to the realm of fantasies, ideals to the bin of impossibility or impracticability—or tomorrow. Most of you hide ongoing hankerings, gripes, and grudges when you have failed. You are fixated on a self-righteous litany toward people and events because they did not behave as they "should have" or "could have."

People do ride roughshod over your aspirations, your feelings, and your sensibilities. They don't often behave as they should.

But *you* can. As long as your own attitude is subject to the conduct of others, you and your happiness will remain at their mercy. Because of this failing, most of you live lives of shattered dreams, with nothing to do but to stifle your groans and moans of desperation. You chug on with envy for those around you who seem to have "made it." You live a life of mechanical coping, stressed out and starved of recognition. This is the world of the living dead, whining and complaining.

> *"The mass of men lead lives of quiet desperation."*
> —Henry David Thoreau

Most of you are distressed and defeated by your day-to-day disappointments, and all because you have not learned to handle your fear of failure. You get easily depressed and discouraged when you fail, even as these setbacks are necessary to strengthen and steel you to achieve your higher potential. It's paradoxical that **your success depends on how you handle failure**.

I see your viewpoint. The overhanging threat of losing discourages us, and it's important not to lose one's enthusiasm and zeal. I suppose the successful ones have great emotional strength and perseverance.

Yes, and an exuberance that eclipses the frustration of their failures. Your success is not measured by your good luck but by how high you bounce after you hit bottom.

Your ability to handle failure is an ongoing process of discovery and learning, which is totally experiential. You can keep lecturing your kids about how to ride a bike, but they'll truly learn only after a few falls. The old saying goes "a burnt child dreads the fire," and so it is with life. In the simple act of learning how to drink from a cup or glass, every one of you dropped or broke dozens of these before you got it right. Your fruition is in failing and falling first.

> *"Our greatest glory is not in never fall-ing but in rising every time we fall."*
> —Confucius

Education and training helps to hone your skills, but your generals are the soldiers who have been in the front of the fiercest battles and received the deepest wounds.

All of you must perforce survive your own scrapes, and the most successful of you graduate from the "school of hard knocks" as they say. Because good experience is born of bad experience.

How right you are! When I pursued laughteryoga and began assembling groups to make them laugh, I was sometimes ridiculed and humiliated by many people. I had to go it alone with what I believed in. It's sometimes frightening to flounder in the fog, when all you can do is feel your way along.

A while ago I clearly said that you are blessed with intelligence and conscience for a reason: to use these faculties to soar to greater heights. True, your vision will often be clouded by

> *"I will not say I failed 1000 times, I will say that I discovered there are 1000 ways that can cause failure."*
> —Thomas Edison

frustration and failure, but this is what makes life interesting for you. There would be no challenge to your faculties if it were smooth sailing all the way. All the games and activities that tap your skills excite you precisely because there is no certainty of winning every time. In fact there is a winning because there is a losing, and vice versa.

Tell me something, do you enjoy fishing?

I love it! I can spend hours, even days at it.

Do you go fishing because you can't afford to buy the fish you catch?

Of course not! It's about the sport, about finding the right spot, the right bait, perfecting the right reeling-in technique. It's not all luck, you know.

Does it test your skills?

Absolutely. Deep-sea fishing is more grueling, but all fishing is about the excitement of a good catch.

It's about the excitement of prevailing over the elements, of outwitting your prey, of showing off your success.

You're right.

Now suppose fishing were a mechanical and automated activity. You can catch your fish at the press of a few buttons. Would that be exciting?

That'd be boring.

> *"We find no real satisfaction or happiness in life without obstacles to conquer and goals to achieve."*
> —Maxwell Maltz

Exactly! The joy of a win is something to cherish through your own efforts. And this is one more of your trademark traits, because you value the excitement of the chase and the victory only when you do it all on your own, without the direct help of others. So **your best skills are those you learn yourself; you hold dearest what you earn yourself**.

You feel excited when you discover your own unique purpose because *you* made the voyage of discovery. Because in your journey, you charted your own course, worked to your own timetable, weathered your own storms.

You're right. We'd feel dead if we were spoon-fed from birth to death. There'd be no challenge, nothing to achieve, nothing to live for. No excitement, no joy.

Yes. The recognition you earn has a different taste from the one you inherit.

A mountaineer doesn't parachute down to the peak he wants to scale. He trudges wearily with his knapsack up the ravines and slopes. He risks his life and reduces himself to skin and bones, all for the moment of celebration after his conquest. Do you think he triumphs because he's got a superhuman body?

No. His victory is over his mind. He keeps egging his legs on to carry him upward. He blanks out all pain and fatigue.

He blanks me out—his inner devil. I'm the nagging doubts that plague him and test his courage. His only hope is to turn a deaf ear to me.

> *"The harder the conflict, the more glorious the triumph. What we obtain too cheap, we esteem too lightly; it is dearness only that gives everything its value."*
>
> —Thomas Paine

You appreciate the gift of life only because it has both ups and downs for you, a winding path with twists and turns that test your ingenuity and resourcefulness. Your best triumph is when you prevail over your problems, using your own self-taught, self-developed, and self-won skills.

A friend once quipped that sweat and toil seem formidable as a *prospect* but lovely in *retrospect*. That said, I guess you're right. I do prize and cherish whatever I've learned all by myself, in my own time and with the freedom to do as I wanted.

God has created you to live your life through free choice, selecting from the umpteen options you are given, so you can taste all its temptations, let your senses run amok, and then learn to mature. From personal experience, you are to sift the successes from the errors, to learn and grow from the confidence of your good experiences, which are born of bad experiences. You relish your success only when you come through after trial and error, slipping and rising. Your feat is in flourishing after your failures.

God grants you a unique reward when you learn from failures and then use your faculties to fight the odds: a wonderful glow of achievement and victory suffuses you after each hard-won success.

I still don't understand why God had to muddy the waters. Why present us with so many wrong turns and twists to agonize over, to suffer from?

The water is muddy because God wants you to work at cleansing and filtering it to enjoy it. If the water were crystal clear, then there'd be nothing to work at, no seeking, no discovery, no joy.

If your joy comes from defeating the odds, then why do you rue the odds? If you relish the rush of euphoria after solving an intricate problem, they why do you moan and mope about the existence of problems?

Tell me, would you rather be an animal or a human?

> *"It's not that I'm smart, it's just that I stay with problems longer."*
> —Albert Einstein

Of course I'd rather be a thinking and spirited human. That's what I am. Why do you ask?

Because animals lead a life of mechanical survival. They live without a heightened awareness to seek the sublime splendor that only you humans are capable of accessing.

God blessed you with superior senses and skills—the ability to discern the truth from lies, the proper from the improper—and a conscience to follow. God presents you with myriads of opportunities to create and re-create yourself continuously. And he wants this journey of discovery to be fun, which is why you feel great joy when you hone your abilities and overcome your failures. Your fruition and maturation on earth is about coping, bouncing back, discovering yourself and your limitless possibilities.

You're probably right, but yet I do wish that life didn't have so many obstacles. Then it would be easier for us to be happy.

What does happiness mean to you?

For most of us, it's the comfort and security that money brings.

This money mania. Why are you humans so fixated on money?

It's what measures our success. And our good luck too, because some people have the luck to be born rich. I guess money does have a lot to do with our happiness.

As a progression, yes. That's where it ends. Money excites and delights you when you continue to hit new highs, when it is an index of your self-worth. You start out earning $30,000 per year, next year it is $36,000, then $45,000, then $65,000, and in a few years it is $100,000. You feel on top of the world with your achievements, and you suitably surround yourself with the trappings of success. Since your social and cultural upbringing is

Money

Money can buy a good clock
      but not *Time*
Money can buy a great bed
      but not *Sleep*
Money can buy a good book
      but not *Knowledge*
Money can buy sex,
      but not *Love*
Money can buy a position
      but not *Respect*
Money can buy a big house
      but not a *Home*
Money can buy a good doctor,
      but not *Health*
Money can buy lots of blood
      but not *Life*
Money can buy a fine dog
      but only *Love* wags his tail

achievement oriented, your self-worth is at a high. You think the world values, loves, and accepts you because it has recognized you and your success by rewarding you with money.

Now there's a flat year and then another. You're lost. The rising progression is broken, and you become depressed. Your self-esteem is at a low ebb even though your net worth runs into the hundreds of thousands. That's how most financially motivated people live their lives: living high when they are rising stars and down in the dumps when their fresh conquests stagnate. Even as a book entry, your pay packet must keep growing, or you feel that your status is lowered.

As long as the progression is positive, you're happy, but once it dips downwards, you worry.

Look at the excitement of the lowly garbage collector who is given a raise from $25,000 to $30,000 per year. This increase in $5,000 does nothing to uplift the millionaire's mood because the relative progression is small.

I do agree that money's not everything. But surely it's the leading precondition to one's happiness?

Money works to promote happiness only to a limited extent, in the progression from abject poverty to a physically comfortable situation. This is what your latest happiness research ratifies. Further money after that yields diminishing returns and feeds the ego. Your success breeds affluence, which creates permanently raised expectations of experiencing the "wow" of achievement all the time.

A 1995 research study by Silbereisen, Smith, and Fombonne has concluded that despite the sharp rise in living standards, Americans today are little or no happier than earlier generations. These studies also prove that if your income doubled, you would initially be delighted, but soon get used to all the extra money and then revert back to your original state of satisfaction. A new survey of some four thousand Americans by your leading academics yields some intriguing results about the specific activity during which people feel happiest. The standout results pointed to "engaging leisure and spiritual activities."

Engaging activities pertained to those where you're engrossed, not stressed. And your spiritual acts are food for the hunger of your heart to find meaning. Many impoverished people in third world countries are happier than their wealthier counterparts. It's because spiritually they are more at peace with themselves.

Money is not the most important ingredient of your happiness.

How can you say that? What about those born rich—aren't they happier, luckier?

How rooted you are to your earthly, finite thinking! Your happiness has little to do with your money. It is an illusion created by your perception of having bettered your condition in some way: materially, emotionally, egotistically. When you have furthered your situation or status, it gives a boost to your ego. This you label as your happiness.

Oh. I thought that many of us are born luckier, happier.

You live with the notion that some of you are served more happiness on your plates than others. This is a rose-colored interpretation of your reality. Nothing could be further from the truth.

Your earthly happiness as you call it is fleeting, a mirage that is visible one moment, gone the next.

How can you say that happiness is fleeting? I know lots of people who enjoy continued happiness.

Your definition of happiness is the "fulfillment of desires." But having fulfilled your desires, there is only emptiness ahead. A hungry stomach will be overjoyed with a feast, but must growl again to find satisfaction. A player having won a difficult game relishes the moment of victory only fleetingly; he becomes beset with replicating and repeating the victory again and again. A mathematician may spend days over a particularly intricate puzzle, and his joy knows no bounds upon solving it—only to yearn for another puzzle sooner or later.

Then there is psychological adaptation to your toys and trinkets: the new sports car, the diamond necklace, the bigger TV, the latest gadget. You delight in playing with your new super-toys, but not for long. You soon digest the wonder and joy, and then the "habituation effect" sets in. You get used to the new situation, and the elation is replaced with boredom. You constantly need new toys to feed your fancy. In the world of material and ego pursuit, what is sought today is on tomorrow's garbage heap. A new car is a new toy and gives off good feelings only for a limited period, after which psychological adaptation sets it, the euphoria settles down, and you set your sights on a new, higher high. Today's happiness is tomorrow's history.

Once you've fulfilled your desires, or reached your illusory happiness, you find ways to be miserable again. That is your nature—the way you were built. Elation is a pinnacle, not a plateau. Your fun is in the scaling and climbing. Oh yes, you're thrilled with success, but only long enough to wish to repeat the thrill of fresh conquest.

You mean our happiness is doomed to start with?

> *"The word 'happiness' would lose its meaning if it were not balanced by sadness."*
>
> —Carl Jung

That's correct. Your jubilation and rejoicing is momentary, in fact self-destroying. It wishes to culminate the experience so as to repeat it and relive it. Oh sure, there is happiness in winning through a challenging situation. But the moment it's over, so do you descend from this peak experience. Now there is anxiety about repeating the performance, a fear.

So it is with your sexual arousal. Your race towards a climax is self-destructive too, because it ends the experience. Your happiness is a peak to be scaled again and again, and therefore it is perforce passing and momentary.

You have a desire, an urge. You sweat and suffer, undergo hardship to satisfy your wants. This misery and suffering is your impetus to work harder to better your condition, so as to repeat the fulfillment experience. You tug and toil, slog and strive to gratify a desire and with luck, maybe one day you will even succeed. To start the happy-unhappy cycle all over again.

I never looked upon happiness the way you're describing it. Can't we be continually happy in some way? I'm sure if you hit the jackpot, then you can be happy forever.

For ever is more like for a year. Research by your Dr. David Myers has shown that your lottery winners enjoy increased levels of happiness only temporarily and find new worries to lean on within less than a year after having won their prizes. Conversely, the people who undergo traumatic tragedy—amputation, bereavement, great personal and financial loss—also return to their original pre-tragedy preset "happiness point" in less than a year.

The great truth of life is that **in misery lie the seeds of happiness and in happiness the seeds of misery**.

I find that hard to believe. So many wealthy people I know look so happy all the time.

Ha! You envy the wealthy because you think they have the best of everything. In truth, the happiness of the wealthy is greater only in your perception of it.

How can rich people possibly be unhappy when they can afford to fill almost every need?

You measure happiness by how many desires you can fulfill. The sad truth is that your desires spring from the blueprint of living supplied by the larger society around you—not only the Joneses next door. The benchmark of how happy you are is derived from your TV and media, which defines your position in society. You gape and gawk at the actors and actresses of Lifestyles of the Rich and Famous, and this gives birth to your desires. Your society forces you to compare yourself with your siblings, your neighbors, your classmates. Your desires and subsequent happiness are molded by the expectations of your parents and society around you.

The Polynesian native living an idyllic life in Tahiti considers happiness as shelter from a typhoon, not the latest game console. Many provinces in the world are not covered by international television and the desires it spawns. The ultimate prize for people here is not the gadget-laden car, but something closer to home and their imaginations—maybe just a good catch while hunting.

You mean most of our wants are proposed by the media?

Only your biological, bodily needs spring from within you. The rest are suggested by the media or your society. The birth of a want is when you see it advertised, or when somebody else has it. Your society triggers not only your desires but places you on a level of status in life relative to that of others.

You feel happy as long as you are in an active, rising progression of status. And sad once the progression of rising wealth and fame stagnates or turns into a regression. That, too, my dear, is the nature of the beast.

Much of your perception of happiness has to do with the trinkets and trophies you amass in your journey of life, vis-à-vis others in your society. Whatever the level of wealth and worldly success you achieve, you will stay within the narrow confines of your happy-unhappy cycle.

You mean our happiness is *relative* to something else, in some way?

> "A wealthy man is one who earns $100 a year more than his wife's sister's husband."
>
> —H.L. Mencken

Yes indeed. Relative to your wealth and achievements of yesterday, and relative to that of others. Your famous author, Gore Vidal, summed it up when he once said that "it is not enough to succeed, others must fail."

Happiness for you humans is a progression of relativity, never a constant—a progression of happy-unhappy sensations in different settings and circumstances.

So happiness is simply the sensation of fulfilling one's desires?

Yes. The more obsessed you are with the fulfillment of your desires, the more impatient you are to satisfy them. These are the days of instant gratification.

What do you mean?

Instant noodles, instant coffee. Fast food, fast cars. Quick money, quick ulcers. Shotgun relationships with shotgun endings.

I'm getting confused. Where and when does one get happy?

Today. Right here and now.

There's a lot of New Age-speak going around that talks about living in the here and now. What does it mean?

If you're focused on past events, chances are you'll be dwelling on your failures, problems and inadequacies, dashed dreams. Your happiness of the present moment is marred by these regrets.

But happy memories can bring a smile to your lips too.

Sure. Though you recall unhappy memories more easily and oftener. When you've lost something, you whine and cry for hours and days, but a good luck windfall is quickly digested and forgotten.

What do you mean?

Just that you find it easier to retrieve and mull over bad memories or bad outcomes. The researchers Phra Phaisan Visalo and Atika Achakulwisut asked a large group of people to recall the happy and unhappy events in their lives during the past ten years. Most of the people remembered the bad times but couldn't recall the good ones.

That's interesting!

The unhappy "happenings" were stretched by the participants to include their list of complaints about their money, the world, the weather, people they related to, their health, their bad luck, dashed hopes…

Oops!

The research concluded that you have a greater attention and memory for negative things. When you dwell on negative outcomes, your matching emotions of regret, fear, loss are

> "*You can clutch the past so tightly to your chest that it leaves your arms too full to embrace the present.*"
>
> —Jan Gildwell

negative too, and you sink into depression. You are gripped by emotions which are often a blast from the past.

I see what you mean. I guess the way we feel right now is tempered by our past feelings.

Or a fear of the uncertain future. Since you so easily dwell on past failures and losses, your perception of tomorrow is also affected and infused with fear. The same fears about what's going to happen to your money situation, the world, the weather, the people you relate to, your health, your luck, your hopes. One way or another, your feelings in the here and now are colored by past or future misery.

So the only real happiness is now, this moment?

Yes. If you can truly be free of fear, free of past emotional baggage, free of the bondage of your ego, then indeed your happiness is right here, right now, in this moment.

Think carefully. The now is pure experience, pure awareness. It is up to you to inject good or bad feelings into this now. You can infuse past emotional baggage or fears of the future into it, but if you can avoid this interference into the now—then now is full of happiness.

It's a decision you make to be joyful.

This reminds me of the time when the Dalai Lama was being interviewed by a reporter, who asked the great sage to recall the happiest time of his life.

How did the Dalai Lama respond?

The Lama said that in all his seventy-plus years, the happiest moment of his life was right here, right now, in that moment, talking to the reporter.

Aha! Now you see it, now you don't!

So it is. I guess we all have our unique interpretation of what makes us happy.

But you cannot escape the reality of its duality, its on-off, on-off progression: happy one moment, unhappy the next. Happiness as you know it—the fulfillment of desires—is never long-lasting. It is doomed from the start. A while ago, I showed you how God depends on the anti-God for his existence, and so does happiness depend on unhappiness for its existence.

It is psychologically impossible for you humans to stay in a constant state of happiness or euphoria, because your happiness is self-erasing.

The people who look happy may be masking untold pain and sorrow. The poor and rich are equally caught up in a progression of happy-unhappy, happy-unhappy sequences.

Unless, of course, your happiness is somehow set free from this cycle of happy-unhappy, unless you can learn to liberate yourself in some way from your past emotional baggage and your worries for the future.

How can this be done?

By banishing the ego, which is present every time you feel any kind of fear, or hear yourself saying "that's mine!"—the voice of attachment.

Where there is ego, there is attachment, and where there is attachment, there is fear. And where there is fear, there cannot be love, and where there is no love, there is misery.

The egoless state is devoid of attachment. There is no yours and mine, no "I'm bigger, you're smaller."

> *"Ego has a voracious appetite, the more you feed it, the hungrier it gets."*
> —Nathaniel Bronner

It is no small wonder that God has made the pinnacle of your sexual orgasm as a total loss of ego. It is described as "mind-blowing" because that is what it does—it blows the ego away! Pure sensation, pure consciousness.

What is this "egoless" state you speak of?

A state when you are free of mind chatter and clutter. Your thoughts are racing this way and that; your emotions are fighting with each other for space. Your ego, which creates the walls between you and others, blocks you from the joy of boundaryless feelings. An egoless state is when you have no awareness of time and space. There is no past and future, only this present, this consciousness of the moment.

So that's what makes the sexual orgasm so special?

Your orgasm is so deep and intense because you're suddenly released from the bondage of your ego. You forget who you are at the height of the act. You lose any distance between old and young, rich and poor, black or white. You stop *thinking*. You experience a momentary thoughtlessness and lose yourself and your ego during sexual orgasm. You feel pure sensation, pure awareness, untainted by the distraction of your possessions, power, and prestige. If only for the instant of release, you have lost yourself to a different world of pure perception.

Your ecstasy is because you are suddenly unshackled from the baggage of your ego. Though only for a moment, you feel liberated, in touch with your inner self.

Is that why we desire sex so much? Isn't sex also a biological release?

Yes, indeed. Animals enjoy sex too, but for them it's only for procreation, not recreation. You humans have higher intelligence but an ego to match. Sex for you is a pinnacle of bliss, when you've transcended your ego. For this reason, sex for you is more than biological—it's also a spiritual experience of pure consciousness, fleeting though it is.

Your attraction to sex is commanded by an urge to re-experience this egolessness and timelessness again and again.

Is there a way to experience a permanent orgasm?

You're obviously fascinated by and fixated on sex. A sexual orgasm is a peak, a culmination of your body, mind, and soul rushing for release. A great gush to be lived and felt as such.

The permanent orgasm cannot be physically sexual because the body stands depleted and must recharge. So your everlasting orgasm has to come from the mind and soul alone.

This spiritual orgasm as a lasting ecstasy is possible when you have cancelled out the ego for longer periods of time.

Is this possible?

Yes, when you are not emotionally attached to the outcome of your actions. When you are disconnected from what may happen, and the result may go either way. This is possible when spiritual gratification is your only objective.

You got a glimpse of this you during your giving and meaning.

When you have learned to decouple your ego from your mind, it's like a spell is cast on you that keeps you continually excited and glowing: a constant state of arousal and awareness, an ongoing orgasm of your inner self.

Wow! Are there any real people who can experience an everlasting orgasm?

A Buddhist monk was once asked whether he missed sex. He said how can you miss it when you're coming all the time!

I like your sexy style. I'd gladly follow in the footsteps of your Buddhist monk, if only to "come all the time"! That's a big motive to practice spirituality. Are there any quick and easy ways to do this?

Spirituality is an experience of your inner being—an ongoing act of discovery. By staying in tune with your conscience to do the good thing, the helping thing, the healing thing. You described the feelings well when you spoke of finding meaning in your life.

I get it. I believe that only in *giving* are you truly *getting* your happiness. Are there any other routes to spirituality?

Many roads lead to the same destination, all with the common thread of banishing fear from your heart. The giving in spirituality—to others, to the community, to nature—is a selfless act. You are happy because you are giving. Period. This is true whether or not the giving produces tangible results. And therefore, you are not attached to the results of your giving. You have banished your ego, banished fear.

Now you are ready to open your heart to the superior spiritual experience of new, heartwarming sensations, a new awareness, and an elevated state of consciousness.

Aha! So the important thing is to get rid of fear.

Yes, because ego is supported by fear. People can be smug about their biceps or their beauty or their wealth and power. This is a raw deal, however, because all boasting is born of fear, self-doubt, and spiritual poverty. Your trinkets and trophies have a short shelf life and can be taken away. The more precious and rarified they are, the more they survive on fear for their value and worth. The bigger your sandcastle is, the greater your loss if it's gone, and the greater your fear. The higher you sit, the harder you fall.

I suppose when you're giving, there's no competitive urge, no barometer of success, and therefore nothing to fear. It's easy to be dissociated from the outcome.

Exactly. When you're helping and healing others, then you are captivated and immersed in this. You find enjoyment in the process, and the outcome is immaterial. This is what your inner heart feeds on to reach higher realms of consciousness: a state of bliss, a continuum of heightened awareness that unveils the mystery, wonder, excitement, and adventure of being alive. This is a world beyond conventional happiness because it is not based on the formula of fulfillment of desires.

You're so right! The elation from giving, or from finding meaning, does not hop back and forth from happy to unhappy in fits and starts. Instead, there's a continuous, lasting glow.

Do you know why? It's because when you give, it is done unilaterally as an act of love and care, and is therefore rid of fear. Your mind is a faculty of reasoning and equally a faculty of distortion. When you give, you are mindless to the outcome, and therefore you have unfettered yourself from this anxiety. You have risen above your mind and entered into a new, higher state of soul-consciousness.

This is the door opened by the act of giving or pursuing purpose.

When you are in the higher, purer state of helping out with God's work, then your euphoria is unshackled from fear. It is the only time that your happiness is unpunctuated and unbroken—at a continuous higher level.

I get it! You're right, Mr. D. My understanding of the joys of giving was indeed crude and incomplete. You've opened up new horizons to these joys. The warm glow of *giving* is not a point or peak, but a plateau at a higher level. This fits in with what you said about the continuing orgasm.

Why the act of giving is accompanied by good feelings is because giving presupposes abundance. Whether or not you have enough, when you give, in a way, you're thanking God for having enough to give. And your thanks is out of gratitude for the abundance on which love prospers.

Conversely, stinginess is founded on feelings of paucity, which is actually the consciousness of not having enough, and is fear-driven. So when you're giving, you're acting from compassion and reinforcing an affirmation of gratitude for the abundance God has bestowed on you. This instantly lights up your heart from within with happiness and love.

Is this how abundance is connected to detachment?

To a large extent. When you feel a great abundance surrounding you, it does not matter what or how much you are giving because the great abundance will not make you any poorer.

When your happiness springs from compassion, love, and abundance, then it turns into long-lasting bliss. Unlike material pursuits—which must end in defeat—spiritual life is an eternal adventure. You experience a unique satisfaction unparalleled by any experience of the mundane world.

You're right. Nothing beats the lasting high that comes from *giving*. It's a steady and prolonged state of wonderment, rapture, and euphoria.

I congratulate you! Indeed, I rather like your raw sparkle, and must commend you in discovering some inner joy too. This satisfaction and serenity is superior to the shallowness of earthly happiness as the world knows it.

It's kind of you to say this, and I greatly value your compliment. I'm grateful to the elements and to God that I've discovered a happiness that exceeds the duality that you've described. In my humble way, the sense of meaning I've found in my life has opened up a whole new world for me: a world of affinity, affection, and connectedness to God. I feel more at ease and at peace than the people I see around me, and I feel lucky to have discovered this new dimension of life.

Indeed you are fortunate. But tell me, your laughter activity, is it a skill or hobby or something more to you?

It's my life now. When my laughter participants quiz me on what I do in my real-life day job, I quip that laughter is my real job. My day job of textile design is by the way and part-time. Isn't that strange?

It's not strange. It's the truth. Can you guess why?

I suppose because when I'm actively spreading laughter, it's the only time I feel *alive*: animated, excited, and vibrant; all systems *on* and on the *go*; joyful to the extreme.

Can you describe why and how your spreading laughter has become more rewarding and valuable than your other work of textile design?

It's as if I exude a deep sympathy, a great warmth, for anybody and everybody. I experience a profound purity of being. I feel cleansed and cured by the almost cosmic connection to the flow of the world. It's a private experience, but priceless.

Is it not true that it was your soul that led you into your laughter work?

Absolutely. My soul was swept away by the mysterious excitement and joy of bringing laughter into others' lives.

What does soul mean to you?

The soul for me is my innermost node of sensation, where feelings are felt.

> *"...a soul, a spark of the never-dying flame that separates man from all the other be-ings of earth!"*
>
> —James Fenimore Cooper

Not a bad description, because your soul is your inner heart, your inner self and spirit. It's where you feel the deepest of your emotions. And that, my dear, is another nuance to your nature. You are different from animals because you have a soul, and **your ultimate happiness lies in finding, feeling, and feeding your soul**.

Aha! So there's no beast in "the nature of the beast," because we have souls.

Beastliness is your lower nature; rising above it is your higher one. Your ongoing search for happiness has but one goal, one destination, and that is to touch and elevate your soul. All your other experiences are but early links of a sequence which leads to one final end. And that is soul-consciousness.

So all roads, all the inroads, lead to *one* destination!

Yes indeed. Soul-centered people have lifted themselves from the quicksand of the body and ego, and appreciate the world for its great abundance. Such people forge ahead to live out their

> "*Of the three prerequisites of genius; the first is soul; the second is soul; and the third is soul.*"
> —Edwin P. Whipple

dreams, to actualize themselves. As souls, they have found their purpose, their meaning, and something beyond earthly happiness.

You mean that soul-consciousness is the one and only goal to pursue?

Yes, it is the one and only purpose of your lives, the highest goal above all goals. Be conscious of what appeals to your soul, and you cannot go wrong. Your soul strives for true peace, and this can come to you by following the dictates of your conscience, not religion. Your conscience seeks to be stilled, to be free from remorse and guilt. It guides you into your giving, which gratifies your soul.

Wow! I've already spoken to you about how I followed my soul when it was captivated by laughter. I listened to it. And that began a kind of spiritual journey.

A do-it-yourself, go-as-you-please journey. It is not the discovery of more earthly pleasures, but self-discovery. The journey is into yourself, and the destination is getting to know your soul better.

Are there some easy ways to go about the journey? What is there to do?

Your thoughts are on doing, but this journey is about being. It's not about what you achieve or amass, but what you become.

Your Western world is hell-bent on controlling, conquering, and taming things and forces external to you and your surroundings. You even want to control the weather and travel to Mars. But the greatest journey of the soul is to comprehend and conquer your internal self. The inner peace that your soul needs is not outside you, in the world of possessions, but inside you.

> *"Everyone thinks of changing the world, but no one thinks of changing himself."*
>
> —Leo Tolstoy

What do you do to find your inner joy?

As a habit, you go for outer things, thinking they'll bring you inner joy and happiness. But in real life the reverse holds true. You first find inner joy, inner peace, and satisfaction, and then all the outer things to support it show up.

Your biggest challenge is not the goings-on in the outer world but understanding and conquering your inner world. That is where you will connect to your inner spirit, where physics will merge with metaphysics and you will understand creation for what it is.

I'm fascinated by what you've said. It describes my feelings perfectly. Ultimately, we all want to satisfy the longings of the soul. I've succeeded to some extent here. I get it now. Soul-consciousness is where our journey ends.

My dear chap, it's where your journey begins.

CHAPTER 7

SOULAR ENERGY

 You really know how to provoke my interest, Mr. D. Just when I digested the meaning of your words, you said something so novel and intriguing.

Ha-ha! I have no wish to provoke you. We can end this journey, this conversation, right now if you wish.

Oh no! You said the journey *begins* here. My curiosity is piqued. You've got to go on.

Great. We were talking about your soul-consciousness, how it is the one final end of your life on earth—to get in touch with your soul.

You arrive at this state in a certain progression, a sequence. Your lower-order happiness comes first, sated by maximizing the sensory experience: You consume good food and wine. Your sexual urges are set to the sexploration mode, seeking the most intensive and extensive experience. You adorn yourself in finery and spread your wings into bigger and fancier nests, because next is your need to be loved, appreciated, and admired. See the sequence: from body-centric you become mind-centric and then ego-centric. You hanker for higher levels of social esteem and you become fixated upon this goal. You become politicians for climbing to socially higher levels in your family, your neighborhood, your workplace, your social groups.

You make it seem ulterior.

There's nothing wrong with what you do. It's the early budding of your personality, a maturation process from the age of discovery to a stage of realization and responsibility, a step-by-step unfolding of your higher purpose. Once you've experienced these desires, you rise to a search for meaning to your life. This is when you become soul-centric.

That's neatly put, but there's one thing that continues to bug me here.

What's that?

How do you reconcile the lower-order needs with soul-consciousness? The image of a loving, caring soul I have is someone above human urges, cloaked in a pure white cape of selfless giving. Somehow this doesn't sit right with my conscience when a part of me is aggressive and acquisitive.

I'll respond to your inner turmoil shortly. First, it's a good idea to look at where you stand in your process of evolution. Here's where you'll find the dots that will soon connect to form the picture you seek. Patience, my dear.

That's fine with me. I'm loving every minute of this talk. Let's carry on.

A while ago, you so eloquently spoke of your finding meaning as being a higher plane of existence. From this high plane, everything else on earth appears smaller. So it is with your food and sex and finery. All of these needs, including those that cater to your ego, appear smaller and smaller from a greater height. When you evolve as a soul, these longings become less and less significant in your higher realm of soulful existence.

Indeed, your description of *soul* is very intriguing. It's something to seek within yourself.

Liken yourself to a fruit layered with outer covering, say as a coconut. You must painstakingly peel off the husk and bark, bit by bit, to reach the kernel. That's when you find your soul. A physicist would put it in nuclear jargon, whereby all physical matter is reduced to atoms that elude being seen or touched. And yet atoms are the nucleus of all matter and are energy powerhouses. So it is with your soul.

I'm overwhelmed by the simplicity of what you just said. But I guess only a few of us can reach for the essence of our souls.

That may be so, but all of you have the capability. I marvel at the great gifts you humans are born with: great mental and emotional strength in times of calamities, a formidable fortitude of spirit when you are challenged. When you exercise these strengths, you can exceed the boundaries of your physical limitations.

You've hinted at that before, that God wants us to use our capabilities to the full. My question is, for what end? Is it just to prove that it can be done?

The end of your toils is not the end. The end, or purpose, of your maturation process is a new beginning, the dawn of a new direction in your life leading to fresh fulfillment and a more complete contentment. This is what happens when you've satisfied your senses and are ready for a deeper understanding of the world and yourself.

You did say that we enjoy taxing our abilities. But as a way forward, I'm still sad that our satisfaction has to come through suffering. God loves us so much and wants us to enjoy the world to the fullest, but still heaps hurt and heartache on us. So many experiences turn sour on us, and some of us get more than our fair share of misery and misfortune.

God wants you to experiment and grow from worldly experiences, both good and bad. It is your nature to shy away from anxiety, distress, and pain, when these are the very pillars upon which your ultimate triumph is built.

My question is, why are some of us exposed to more suffering than others?

That is your perception of your reality and not God's fact. Generally speaking, each of you humans is born into a level playing field with quite the same five senses of hearing, sight, smell, touch, and taste. All of you are exposed to more or less the same amount of good and bad chances, advantages, and adversities. How you react to your situation and use your inborn resources is up to you. Many of you blame each other. Or you blame circumstances and fall out of the journey at some point. You become angry and impotent with your situation because you're wide awake to your so-called ill luck and misery, but asleep to your potential and good fortune.

Some time ago, I talked about how your success depends upon how you handle failure. This applies both to your material and spiritual success. Learn from your failures, rise up every time. Put in your best.

So God wants us to do our best during our lifetime on earth, before we die.

You are fixated upon your mortality, whereas in truth you are an immortal soul that comes down to earth from time to time.

Reincarnation! Are you suggesting that it's real?

Before I answer that, what exactly is the soul and what does it want?

I suppose it's an inner voice within us that lives in our hearts and is tempered by our conscience.

Not bad. Conscience is your inner guide of good and bad, apt and inapt. Your conscience hurts when you do something against it and lights up when you reward it with a righteous act.

> *"Intuition is a spiritual faculty and does not explain, but simply points the way."*
> —Florence Scovel Shinn

Add to this instinct, which is drawn from your intuition, a sixth sense. Repeated intuition, or a foreboding or premonition or inborn hunch to react in a certain way, is instinct. It cannot often be explained in words or by cold logic but is conditioned by ongoing experiences.

Together, the two make up your soul. Living, renewable instinct and conscience.

Is that how you define the meaning of *soul*?

Broadly speaking, yes.

Hmm. So instinct is some sort of storage tank of all felt emotions? Or is it a storehouse of thoughts?

Your brain is a microprocessor computer where you store your memories. Instinct is the emotional upshot of experiences and lives in your heart where it touches and tinges your soul.

That's fascinating! What does a soul want?

Your soul, which lives in your heart, craves to maximize the experience of joy and peace to higher and higher levels—this is why it is here on earth. It craves love, which as I said leads to the experience of God. The soul takes your body as a vehicle of the five senses of sight, touch, smell, sound, and taste. Only through these senses can the soul find the joy and fulfillment it seeks.

Ah, so that's why my own soul ran off—to find deeper joy and peace.

As a first step to test the waters and its limits, your body fulfills its cravings to gorge on the most intense and diverse experiences that are possible to digest through your five senses. To see all there is to see, taste all there is to taste, and sense whatever there is to sense through your hearing, smell, and touch. You tend to tip into overindulgence with sugars, food, and drink, and the compulsion to maximize the sexual experience. Most of you devote your entire lives to the pursuit of sensory gratification, or hedonism, and look no further.

There's nothing wrong with having a good time, to seek out and maximize the pleasures that life offers. You said so yourself.

Nothing wrong. Except that the road remains only half traveled, with your life half lived. Your life is incomplete because the best pleasures go untasted, devoid of any depth of emotion and soulfully barren. Come on, we've been over all that. You and I have talked at length about the higher rewards of soul-consciousness.

I'm only trying to reconcile soul-consciousness with the enjoyment of life's attractions.

This is a maturation process. Your sensory thrills are a phase to rise from. You can enjoy, relish, and revel in these gifts that God has bountifully bestowed on you. The tragedy is when you become fixated and ensnared in these lures of maximizing the sensory stimulation.

Your next evolutionary stage is seeking pleasure from the act of control and power. This is your ego, also a trap. You have conquered climate and space, but your ego is unconquerable. For most, your ego is your identity, because you become obstinately assertive when somebody steps on your ego. Your ego only blocks the flow of energy into your lives.

But your soul is more than your body. It is made up of your instinct and your conscience, which is not stilled and satisfied through the bodily sensory ride. It wants more.

What more does the soul want?

Deeper, lasting realms of ecstasy and euphoria, which sensory thrills can't provide. Lasting fulfillment is possible only by catering to your conscience.

> *"The only tyrant I accept in this world is the still voice within."*
>
> —Gandhi

Don't we all listen to the voice of our conscience?

Many on earth simply develop their instinct to further their material and political objectives, and turn a deaf ear to their conscience.

Can you give some examples?

There is many a tale of the high-powered tycoon who unscrupulously plots and plunders for personal profit. Or the corrupt politician with passionate speeches who will sell his mother for added power and prestige. It is "me first, me bigger, me better," to the detriment and disadvantage of hundreds or thousands, or the world at large. There are many whose urge for one-upmanship often requires them to sacrifice the dictates of their conscience for selfish gain. Such are the ones who enjoy material and political success on earth but are unable to elevate and enrich their souls.

Don't you think these examples are extreme?

The examples may be dramatized, but look for the same patterns and traces in your own life, when you have stretched your scruples for money or self-interest. As a real estate broker, do you truthfully put across the pros and cons, or do you suppress some facts to close the deal? Can you truthfully say that you wouldn't hide a bit from the tax man given the opportunity?

While touring a third world country, don't you feel a twinge of guilt at wantonly wasting food in front of impoverished beggars?

You're right. I feel guilty when I suppress my conscience. But come on, it's impossible to be conscientious all the time.

When you increasingly reject the voice of conscience, it becomes wounded. Conscience is the monitor of intuition and instinct, which all together make up your soul. When you silence your conscience, you suppress, hurt, and trap your soul too. You try to appease your soul by clothing it in finery, overfeeding it with conspicuous consumption. The feudal lords of medieval times lived a life of great luxury at the expense of their indigent subjects. But they lived ignorant, aimless, and empty lives, their consciences and souls dulled into a stupor by their debauchery and depravity.

I suppose your conscience does prick you when you're doing something that's socially unjustified.

So many of you shrug off the voice of your conscience and douse your guilt by overfeeding your senses or your ego, all to escape in some way the pangs of self-reproach. But when you ignore your conscience, its howl is heard in your heart as compunction, remorse, repentance, and ruefulness. Your soul becomes a troubled and trapped soul. It stops growing, stops evolving.

You're implying that the pangs of conscience are some sort of guilt trip. I can share your views where the underlying emotion is guilt, but I can't agree that success, money, and power should bring guilt. If I can get these, I can go to my grave quite fulfilled.

There is nothing wrong with success, which should be enjoyed and cherished. Money and power are to be relished too, provided that you do not morally compromise your conscience. There can be no fulfillment if you have bound, gagged, and blindfolded your conscience. Can you enjoy your feast of caviar and champagne in an African country hit with famine, with some starving children looking on? And would you enjoy your ride in a palanquin held up high by emaciated beggars? Would you grab the bus seat even as a hunched and hobbling lady tried to take it? And would you splash around in your five-hundred-gallon Jacuzzi unfazed while there's a drought going on and water is rationed?

I suppose if you're conscious to the cry of the world around you, then you perforce have to give in to your conscience.

It is not enough to be conscious. You must be conscientious. Repeated, reinstated intuition becomes instinct. In the same way, repeated, reinstated conscience becomes your conscientiousness.

Wow! That's a mouthful! I'll take some time to chew on it. For a start, I believe *conscious* means being awake.

Awake and aware of who you are, what you are, and why you are—with what purpose you are. That is your correct consciousness vis-à-vis your surroundings and yourself.

The only souls at peace with themselves are the ones who keep their conscience as a long-term friend, guide, and philosopher. They easily move from one joy to another and seek out the highest, most profound joys that go beyond satisfying only sensory cravings. By listening to their inner voice, these souls reap the deeper rapture of relating to the world with concern for it.

Conversely, the body that runs after only sensory pleasures becomes the graveyard of the soul.

Ultimately all souls gravitate toward love. Animals also have the five senses but don't overindulge them. Only humans overload the senses to become overweight, oversexed, overwhelmed with their super-toys. As humans, your cry for love, respect, and admiration manifests itself in the lust for possessions and power. Humans forget that the purest love springs from compassion, which alone nourishes the soul.

> *"Nothing can cure the soul but the senses, just as nothing can cure the senses but the soul."*
> —Oscar Wilde

Some time ago you talked about a euphoric bliss that dwells upon those who give, who have found meaning and therefore a connection with God. This is when the soul is truly healed, nourished, rejuvenated, and reenergized. This is the nectar of perennial bliss and what souls strive for. This act of purification is the ultimate goal of each soul and really the purpose of its journey on earth.

And then our souls live on forever?

Yes. **As a soul, you never die and are never born. Your soul knows no time and space and lives in a continuum where only love exists. It is an ongoing repository of instinct ripened and refined through many lives of experience on earth.**

Up there in the soul world, the soul feels and even communicates, but telepathically. It visits earth from time to time in a physical body via its birth.

I've felt the soothing salve of soul-consciousness, but I'm still at sea about reincarnation. How does that work?

Think of the human existence on earth as a video recording with an erase or reset button. At death the physical body is gone and memories of its existence on earth are also cleared, erased. The soul is neither the body, nor memories of events, feelings, and emotions. The soul retains only the emotional essence, or compressed emotional instinct, derived from experiences. This is what lives on. With each birth, the soul is merely a traveler on earth, sent to ripen, refine, and enrich itself each time.

At every birth, the soul takes up a human body with its past life video recording erased and the memory banks reset and empty. With no

> "*Life is the soul's nursery.*"
> —William Makepeace Thackeray

memory of a past life, during its time on earth the soul drinks in all the joys of discovery, through childhood to adulthood. It tastes and savors life's experiences through the five senses. The soul lives through both frustrations and achievements. Through free will, it charts its own unique course to find the most intense and lasting joy. The soul thirsts for love and acceptance, which is best experienced through spiritual connection, or soul-consciousness. With intuition and conscience as its tools, the soul develops and refines its spirit of instinct and consciousness.

Why does a soul have to go through this rebirthing?

To re-subject itself to real-life experiences through the human physical senses, to purify itself, to grow spiritually, to accomplish unfulfilled desires from past lives, to complete an unfinished agenda. **The purpose of the**

soul's journey on earth is to perfect itself via varied experiences. To strive for ongoing spiritual self-purification as a route to the ultimate lasting joy and bliss.

Surely, with all their wisdom, souls don't need to go through the growth pains and miseries all over again. From up above in heaven they could simply look down on earth and learn from others' experiences?

The soul's visit to earth in a body is not about learning the alphabet or speech or arithmetic, or how to drive a car or work a computer. All these are skills; they are erased and must be relearned.

Souls need to feel firsthand emotions to polish themselves.

A good part of the soul is instinct, which is built on perception and feelings. Feelings in turn come from firsthand experience.

> *"I simply believe that some part of the human Self or Soul is not subject to the laws of space and time."*
> —Carl Jung

Souls need the exposure of life on earth, which alone touches raw nerves and leads to raw emotions, which must be felt. You can't say "don't worry" to a mother on an overnight vigil for a dying child. It is just as meaningless to surround the starving with food and expect moderation and manners. Life on earth is fraught with temptation and distraction at every stage, to understand and rationalize. You'll never know how a beggar will respond to finding a bounty in a lost handbag, unless you actually live in his body with its own dismays, disappointments, and dashed dreams.

You're right. Certain feelings have to be felt firsthand to be understood.

Each new life experience on earth yields firsthand sensations, which flavor the past reservoir of instinct the soul has built up over several lives on earth. New experiences on earth tinge, recolor, and reshape archaic instinct.

For example?

Souls react to earthly challenges depending on their state of evolution. An unpolished soul still struggling to appreciate the value of compassion will grab and brag, whereas a more evolved soul may exercise tolerance and compassion to heighten its sensitivity.

The upshot is that the emotive essence of every experience on earth is unique, used by a soul to heal itself and to redeem and refine itself. It is for this very purpose that souls descend to earth from time to time.

But why must souls come to earth for this firsthand experience?

Because out there in the soul world there is no experience, just a vast vacuum. The experiences of random events on earth serve to mold the soul. To correct, cleanse, and refine it.

But why slip and stumble in life with all the right instincts from previous births?

You don't seem to get it. The soul has instinct and conscience but no memories of a past life. Souls don't carry stock-trading success secrets into a new life because these are skills, not instinct. This is why children don't act in a cold and calculating manner as they come into this world. Children bask in and respond to love, which is their natural state of consciousness relative to the world. They don't hunt and gather what they need, but take in whatever is available. Instinct tells children to laugh, play, and share. Grabbing and grudging are optionally learned later, as secondary responses to deprivation and the fresh, earthly teachings of each life.

Souls live from life to life with the purpose of smoothing out the wrinkles in their being, to light up their consciousness, to continuously define and refine themselves, bit by bit, over a string of lifetimes on earth.

A minute ago, you said souls can get troubled when conscience is silenced. Does instinct also go the wrong way here?

Unfortunately, yes. Victims of abuse suffer till their sobbing falls silent. When somebody's conscience and intuition are trampled upon in his formative years, he undergoes great emotional hurt. In such cases, the giving and taking of hurt becomes hardwired as an intuitive reaction. With a corrupted instinct, these very same people then muzzle their consciences and abuse others. The adolescents who stray into crime reflect early-life traumas or abuse. As children, their cry for love was met with punishment meted out by their near and dear ones. A corrupted instinct leads to corrupted conscience, and the end result is crime without compunction.

How do you heal such people, whose conscience is stifled and instinct is twisted, tainted? Is there a chance for them?

There's every chance, provided the victims of abuse can be shown that they can't change the past and may even have to atone for their past sins. But the future belongs to them to embrace as an educated soul in a new environment. This is how rape victims learn to cope, how drug addicts reform, and how criminals become champions of the law.

Experienced social workers have learned how to rehabilitate society's fallout victims: by restoring love to their feelings and by rebuilding and reconstructing conscience, making it strong enough to overpower their contaminated intuition and instinct. This is a great experience in the evolution of a soul, to conquer fear and hatred with love and hope. The soul is retaught, reprogrammed, rehabilitated. It is re-educated about which urges and reactions to starve and which ones to feed and fortify.

By golly! I can recall many moments in my laughter sessions when someone walked in distressed and depressed, and walked out as an invigorated soul. I'm impressed with the depth of your knowledge. What is the specific agenda of a soul in taking up rebirth?

To enrich itself through earthly experiences. A soul comes into this physical world with noble intentions of using the opportunity for the maximum spiritual upliftment. To evolve in terms of soul-consciousness into a more erudite, wiser soul. Because this alone leads to lasting peace, to bliss.

Does this always happen, and how?

You enter life at point A and hope to exit at point B after completing your life expectancy. Some choose the obstacle course, some the scenic route. Others choose the greater distance between the two points.

I'm totally at sea. Can you just say it in plain words?

I forgot to make allowances for your limited intelligence. I'll put it in simpler language.

Many souls are awake to the world with its infinite opportunities, and transcend the temptations of the senses to purify themselves. Through sharpened sensitivity, sensibility, and alertness relative to the world, these souls reach out for and attain a higher realm of eternal ecstasy, not just passing pleasure.

Other souls get trapped in feeding their senses or their egos, and lose sight of their original purpose in visiting the earthly life. They fail to elevate their conscience via heightened consciousness.

I get it. Not all souls actually follow the purpose of their journey on earth.

All souls are unique because each is at a different level of evolution—of heedfulness and realization vis-à-vis life. At one extreme, the soul without a conscience at all can be likened to a fused bulb. It does nothing to brighten the environment and gains nothing from it either. It gets caught up in one or another trapping on earth and fritters away its chance, or lifetime, on earth.

At the other extreme are souls so enriched and aware that they emit a bright radiance. These are the sages and savants who have from their varied experience on earth discovered the most blissful feelings, gleaned the most. They enjoy super-consciousness—overflowing with love and living in a state of divine bliss. Through compassion and soul-consciousness they further polish themselves during their journey on earth.

I see. And do souls ever die?

No, they're always around and merely wear different clothes. When not on earth, souls float around in a timeless, spaceless vacuum—the soul world we discussed. They exist as invisible specks, archives and repositories of instinct and consciousness, aware of what and where they are but unable to participate in physical experience. Some souls shine brighter than others because they have, over a string of lifetimes, discovered and refined themselves and bloomed into a higher state of flowering, a higher state of consciousness. This is the night sky of evolution, with some invisible stars, some dim stars, and some bright stars.

This word *consciousness* you speak of; it gives a wider meaning to how you feel about how you react to the world—beyond simply being awake.

To be conscious is to be aware and alive. I spoke of your five senses a while ago. You can use them to soak in pleasures and stop there, or heighten the sensitivity of these senses to look beyond your noses into a bigger, more exciting world. You can train your senses to pick up the signals of the needs of others and the world around you. If you learn to practice compassion, you experience more diverse and deeper feelings. As a result, you become alive to the world, ablaze with enthusiasm, fully awake to relish its abundance.

Each soul is unique in its level of consciousness. The more evolved ones have a stronger antenna of reception to tune in to the wonders of the world, a sharper ear to the ground to pick up the harmony of its music. All souls, over several lifetimes, hope to rise to super-consciousness.

You were talking about some sort of progression, covering some distance on earth.

The only chance that souls have of elevating themselves is through firsthand feelings on earth. This is why souls seek rebirth. Some overambitious souls want to pack in the most teasing, trying, and testing times to grow from, and so they choose to be born into adversity, or to be born where trauma will strike them. Other souls are not so adventurous and prefer to be born into security. Many may opt to be born blind, or be put through agony and upheaval, because suffering opens up the pores of compassion. The hardship forces them to cope, learn, and grow spiritually.

And so, my dear, souls choose to be born into certain field conditions. This answers your question about why some people appear to be subjected to greater misfortune than others.

How do you explain lives lost by accidents? Surely souls don't choose to die this way.

The where and how of rebirth is not entirely up to a soul, because God must make the soul's goals achievable. God may wish to offer some souls only a limited time span on earth. The fact of untimely, accidental death on earth is also a learning experience—a particularly important lesson in the complex of life's uncertainties. It highlights God's message to live to the maximum in the here and now. This is also an essential part of creation, which colors with chance lives left to live out their natural years or to be cut short by whatever circumstance.

Go back. Look into your nature. Don't you relish your victories because there is the chance of losing? You feel abuzz with your achievements having survived risk, which makes your triumph so prized and valuable. Risk is what stops you from being rash, from jumping from one rooftop to the other.

This is precisely why God—or His cousin, the anti-God, that's me—litters your path with some dead bodies too.

If God exercises so much control over a soul's course, then where's the free choice?

The free choice is an integral part of creation. Each moment, each experience unfolds afresh for each soul. The excitement of spontaneous discovery is a gift to each soul because predictability is removed, because there is a chance factor in every moment, in every move. The miracle of life as God created it is that once souls enter physical bodies and undergo physical experience, they forget why they came to earth. God wants you to grow spiritually from spontaneous, firsthand experience. For this He designed life as an individual journey of exploration without preset road maps or destinations. With no past-life memory to remind or guide them, most souls succumb to the trappings of sensory or ego gratification and forget to look beyond.

Others are discouraged by early failures and frustrations, and become cynical, skeptical of the ocean of bountiful feelings of warmth, love,

> "The soul is born old, but grows young. That is the comedy of life. And the body is born young and grows old. That is life's tragedy."
> —Oscar Wilde

sharing, and connecting to others. The true nectar of life goes untasted. The feelings that take joy and consciousness to new and uncharted heights often elude the doubtful and disbelieving.

So each life is a fresh reset button in all respects. No memory, no goals. So souls have only instinct to guide them when they come to earth?

Exactly. The instinct gleaned from past lives guides souls to create their own destiny during their lifetime on earth. God's plan is for you to grow from free choice. Past life instinct and conscience does whisper in your ear sometimes, through dreams, longing, and pangs. Many of you do wake up at some point of your lives to pursue purpose and meaning. A random act of kindness and giving yields a new type of joy, which nourishes the soul. A joy that touches your conscience develops a life of its own to seek deeper fulfillment.

What you make of your time on earth is up to you. This is God's way. He presents you with infinite possibilities and methods to uplift yourself. Now do you understand?

I'm getting the picture, and it's fascinating. So souls can actually choose where to be born?

Yes. To undergo the most varied or taxing experiences out of free choice, with the best of intentions.

The divine bliss that souls seek comes only through spiritual growth. This is the ultimate goal of life, not earthly success in the stock market or other misleading achievements. Your triumph on earth is not about being born a millionaire and racking up more of the same; it is in cultivating, developing, and expanding your senses to provide spiritual upliftment.

On a one-hundred-step ladder, it's not about being born lucky at step ninety-eight and moving up to the ultimate one hundredth step. It's about advancing and maturing from whatever rung of the spiritual ladder you're on to a higher level.

For this, you don't need to be born into luxury. Starting life from this vantage point is actually a big handicap to motivation because it deters and distracts you from soul-consciousness. I did say that souls can choose to be born into an easy life or an obstacle course. An easy track does not grow strong legs, but difficult field conditions make you stronger. If you're going to climb a mountain, you need to train on tough terrain. So souls already high up the spiritual ladder of evolution may choose to be born into difficult and demanding conditions on earth. It's a question of extracting the best spiritual mileage out of their journey.

On the same one-hundred-step ladder, there are no limits to how many rungs you can climb in a lifetime on earth. Some souls may actually fall back a few steps. Others may climb only a rung or two. Yet others may tweak their own destiny to devote their entire lives to spiritual growth. They may race up half the ladder or more, like Mother Theresa, like Gandhi.

> *"The soul is placed in the body like a rough diamond, and must be polished, or the luster of it will never appear."*
> —Daniel Defoe

This is how souls evolve, pursue purification and reach toward super-consciousness.

What happens if you've reached the one hundredth step? Are you over and done with life on earth?

First, it's not exactly one hundred steps. This is an example I gave for your limited, lower intelligence to grasp. It's a flexible goal with flexible play. God wants you to pursue your happiness and reach the pinnacle of inner joyfulness. This is how you define the highest rungs of your spiritual staircase. It is the attaining of super-consciousness, or nirvana. You have then conjoined with the Creator to become One with Him and are at a different plane of existence.

So the cycle of birth and death is over?

Yes and no, for a soul is never totally, totally pure and may yet visit earth. But having achieved super-consciousness, you have merged with the Divine Soul and become One with Him. God may yet send you on to earth for a purpose as his messenger, as his emissary.

Is it true that some souls are happier than others? What's happiness for souls?

Earthly happiness is construed as the fulfillment of desires. As we discussed, the gratification is always fleeting, a duality of happy-unhappy. It depends upon misery for its existence.

What souls seek is joy—this is continuous happiness at a higher level based on an inner choice for ultimate peace. Souls reach out for this higher rapture through spiritual enlightenment. Souls are made up of conscience, which culminates into consciousness. If this is at peace, then yes, a soul is happy.

To enter a permanently happy state, your soul is constantly pushing you to seek higher levels of gratification through experience. As you have yourself discovered, the most sublime ecstasy comes from giving, belonging, and doing your best for the world. An immersion into finding meaning is the only act that will soothe a troubled and lost soul. It is the only step that will unfetter you from guilt and distress. This is what leads to lasting happiness.

Many of us lead contented lives on earth the way we are, without the need for any pursuit of meaning or spiritual salvation. Where's the push to pursue soul-consciousness?

There's no pressure of any sort to go off the beaten path. In fact, most of you know of no alternative, nor seek it. You turn a blind eye to the voice of conscience when it does prick and poke you. Your life goes on. But then you miss out on God's bountiful garden. You live a limited life of cloistered pleasures but feel no lasting joy, no bliss. Because you failed to discover your spiritual side.

Your journey on this earth is about participating in a sequence of self-exploration, sometimes tortuous, sometimes straight and simple. You start from hedonism and physical lusting to seeking something better, worthier, and divine. When you learn to identify with your purpose and meaning of life, you come closer to finding unbroken and lasting peace and happiness.

When this happens, you're more focused on the moment, rather than emotions from your past or fears about your future. Your peaceful moments in the here and now stretch. They last longer and longer. This is when you have entered into a state of heightened awareness, a raised level of consciousness. This is your rapture and bliss, a sort of end game to a lifetime on earth, as part of a never-ending journey of spiritual evolution which spans many a lifetime.

Why do some souls manage to educate, cultivate, and elevate themselves on earth, while others seem to falter and fail?

God wants you to use all the faculties he has blessed you with. To rise to your fullest glory, realize your highest potential. Out of free choice and without any compulsion. A wide spectrum of experiences will rain down on you during your life on earth. It is then up to you to choose which way to react, to filter out the negative provocations and cultivate a stronger instinct. Along the journey, conscience will be your guide, provided you heed its word.

And after death all souls go to their soul world? Which is either heaven or hell?

Ha-ha! Heaven and hell! When will you break the bonds of your religious programming? I can't help being amused. What is your picture of heaven and hell?

I guess heaven is full of beautiful gardens, beautiful maidens, no pain and suffering. Full of smiles and laughter. All that is the wine of life. And hell is where you're a prisoner, doing hard labor and suppressed. In a hopeless situation, doing penance for being bad on earth. Suffering every day.

Is that what you learned in your books, in schools, and in your society?

Well, yes. This is what our religions teach. Is my understanding wrong in some way?

Not simply wrong, but foolish and far-fetched. Your heaven and hell are integral to the reward-punishment system of taming your wild nature, and are therefore promoted by your religions.

You mean heaven and hell are figments of our imagination?

Heaven and hell don't exist as large estates on land with boundaries. They are merely your mental and emotional states.

Barely a while ago, you were extolling the virtues, the higher delights of giving and finding meaning. Go back to what you said. You experienced a heavenly feeling from the act of giving back.

Think now of your fabled Midas who spent his time counting his gold. He knew no joy other than the power of possessing more than others. In effect, he became a prisoner to this emotion and could not relish any other aspect of life. That's your living hell.

How can you be so sure that Midas went to hell? That he was unhappy?

Get into the mind and body of Midas for a moment. See how possessed you are with your possessions. You gloat in having more than your neighbor, but the reality is that you live in fear, because you must lock and protect your hoard, fearing that your treasure will be stolen away from you. You suspect everybody in your life as plotting to relieve you of your wealth or in some way ingratiate himself to you. Anxiety, paucity, distrust, fear, worry, and stress have taken the place of love, abundance, calmness, and confidence in your life. You are beset with the threat of loss. Wary and watchful of the world, you both envy and hate your fellow man, who radiates the peace and joy alien to you. Isn't that a kind of hell on earth, even during your lifetime?

I see what you mean. I know many rich people who are equally miserly.

Many of you live your lives in a prison of your own making, locked into a golden cage. When your time on earth is over, you travel as a lost and wandering soul back to the lap of God, regretting your whittled and wasted chance on earth. You are full of remorse and repentance in the vast vacuum of endless, timeless space, in a kind of suspended animation. With only your shame, sorrow, and self-reproach for company. Isn't that a hell in your afterlife too?

Shall I now talk about heaven?

> *"Life is just a chance to grow a soul."*
> —A. Powell Davies

Hmm. I'm getting the picture. On earth people may not know they're in hell, but in the afterlife I do agree it's easier to understand. I'm curious to hear your version of heaven on earth. I like the way you describe things, your clarity.

On earth, if you've tasted the joys of giving and found meaning in your life, then you've left the paucity state and entered abundance. Give a helping hand to a fallen one, and the look in his eyes is more heartwarming than anything else on earth. A sense of feeling wanted and needed casts its own spell of love, which envelops and bathes you in a new type of warmth and joy. If somehow you can bring yourself to feel useful to your fellow man, to nature, or to the world at large, then you experience a new tenderness in your heart, a glow, an ardor and belonging that knows no parallel.

In your own words, you have glorified the act of giving and finding a purpose to your life. You gave a good description, but an incomplete one, because you stopped at the warm glow. In the actual case, this is just a taster, a teaser that God has put before you to tweak you toward finding meaning in your life.

I see what you mean.

If you manage to get in touch with your soul and follow its bidding, you will discover the most powerful ecstasy and rapture known to mankind!

Your explanation has a golden hue, a clarity and essence like no other. I feel I'm transformed, transported into another world, through touching my soul.

Look upon Warren Buffet and Bill Gates, who long ago satisfied their material and ego urges and wanted a higher gratification. They sought and stumbled upon the secret of life's perennial paradise, which comes only from the act of giving, contributing to and being associated with a worthy cause.

Of late, your entertainment stars have also realized that more is actually less, unless they can somehow share their fame with the larger community for its betterment. Oprah Winfrey gives hope to deprived children in Africa and has touched fifty thousand lives. Nicole Kidman champions children's rights and promotes breast cancer research. Bono has worked wonders to persuade the wealthy nations to waive third world debt and is an ardent supporter of free AIDS treatment for the needy. Pierce Brosnan devotes his time to environmental issues, while Salma Hayek and Ashley Judd are part of YouthAIDS. Angelina Jolie performs charity work all over the globe. Her words epitomize her feelings: "…there was a lot about this world that I didn't know. I felt really ashamed and ignorant…it just changed my life."

Just about every human soul craves to find meaning as the route to obtaining spiritual growth, rich and famous people included.

> *"I don't think you ever stop giving. I really don't. I think it's an ongoing process. And it's not just about being able to write a check. It's being able to touch somebody's life."*
>
> —Oprah Winfrey

But the rich and famous can actually contribute much more.

They may be able to sow more, but what they reap is nothing more than the poor cleaning lady, or the indigent retiree, or any other financially strapped person. Each of you is magnetically drawn to seek the fulfillment of your soul, and all of you will put in whatever you can as your investment. Everyday people—housewives, bus drivers, postmen, office workers—all hunger for the heartwarming experience of reaching out to their souls. The poor open up their hearts and efforts, the financially fortunate open up their wallets. And once they've tasted the glow from giving, they're hooked. Worldly acclaim and recognition pale in comparison to the inner ecstasy felt from awakening the soul. This probably explains why 70 percent of all American households donate something to charity every year.

> *"Ridiculous yachts and private planes and big limousines won't make people enjoy life more, and it sends out terrible messages to the people who work for them. It would be so much better if that money was spent in Africa—and it's about getting a balance."*
>
> —Sir Richard Branson

You've got to admire the Americans for their generosity.

It doesn't stop at money. People often donate something more valuable than money, and that's their time. Can you believe that in a typical year more than 60 million Americans volunteer through or for an organization, for a median of fifty-two hours of work? Can you guess why?

An urge to help. I guess this is a very strong need in all of us. But it's puzzling why God had to couch his message in sorrow and suffering.

Sorrow and suffering are necessary to awaken your feelings of compassion. God is not a sadist; he just wants you to look into your own heart, discover your soul. Compassion is a unique feeling, a welling up of empathy and sympathy in you. This opens up the pores of your sensitivity, readies you for the satisfaction of the soul. In your own words, the best getting is giving, so let me utter a few home truths:

> **Give a smile to get a smile.**
>
> **Give respect to get respect.**
>
> **Give your heart to win hearts.**
>
> **Give love to get love.**

Your biggest need is to be needed. And so, your happiness lies in making others happy. You heal yourself only when you heal others.

Most of your unbearable sorrows—a broken heart, the distress of a loved one deceased, great financial loss, a great illness or calamity—all of these become bearable if you focus on the greater suffering of others around you. When you reach out in some way to comfort those in need, you are actually reaching out to your own bleeding heart.

I've actually felt the inner joy that comes from giving. You've now attached a deeper reach, a more profound meaning to this. Giving is a therapeutic experience for the giver.

> *"There is a wonderful mythical law of nature that the three things we crave most in life—happiness, freedom, and peace of mind—are always attained by giving them to someone else."*
>
> —Peyton Conway March

When you connect to your higher purpose, the mundane demands of day-to-day living cease to stress you. Because now you are free from fear, unattached to the outcome of your actions and at your creative best. Now you are charged up with a higher vibration, which silences your mind chatter and connects you with the divine.

There is no turning back now because you are beyond the ordinary fleeting pleasures of existence, into a lasting, heart-warming bliss. Unshackled from fear, anger, envy, and displeasure, you come to embrace both boons and blows, good and bad luck, with equanimity.

You feel alive, creative, energetic, and enthusiastic all the time. You give and receive love freely, and your heart is always warm and connected.

Isn't that a kind of heaven on earth?

Because you look upon others with trust, patience, and love, this is what they reflect to you. Life is a perfect mirror of your feelings and actions, and you find cooperation, tolerance, and patience wherever you go and in whomever you meet. Your soul now resonates at a higher frequency and emits a radiance that is infectious. Is this not a continuing state of joy? Of bliss?

In the afterlife, you feel proud to have experienced a higher realm of consciousness, a deeper bliss. Having shone through your trials and temptations on earth, you become a more elevated soul, a brighter star in the sky. You find it easy to live with yourself.

And that, my dear, is heaven in heaven, or the soul world.

This is fascinating. It seems to unravel the maze of life. Though I can't say that everybody will buy into the reasoning.

I'm here talking to you. I really don't care who buys what. The home truths will come home for anybody seeking them.

You really know all there is to know about us humans. What's left?

Just a few passing observations on what soul-consciousness brings to you.

Isn't this the end of one's purpose in life?

Yes and no. You see, soul-consciousness is a one-way road. Once you touch your soul, you shed the anchor of your body and ego. Your ability to withstand bodily pain and discomfort becomes boundless because the energy that motors you is now something far more powerful than the food of the body, the mind, and the ego. A good example is your Mother Theresa, who could endure endless denial and deprivation.

Your body and mind need food and ego satisfaction as fossil fuels for nourishment. These fuels are exhaustible and only provide temporary gratification.

Your soul thrives on cosmic energy—endless, permanent. As a first cousin to solar energy, your **soular energy** is renewable, clean, and the most powerful energy source that keeps you going forever.

Can you put that into simpler words?

Look around you at your so-called miracles: the cancer patient who got cured by faith; the athlete who broke many a bone but went on to compete in the Olympics; the thousands of people who defied the medical odds to prevail over their bodily boundaries; the many who underwent traumatic tragedy, yet survived. They prevailed and prospered materially, mentally, and emotionally. They rose from abject misery to resounding triumph.

My dear chap, these are not miracles but evidence of the most powerful energy there is on the planet. An energy that heals, electrifies, empowers, and excites like no other.

> "The most powerful weapon on earth is the human soul on fire."
> —Ferdinand Foch

When your thoughts are spiritually pure, or when ruled by the meaning so ably defined by you, then your spirit is plugged into a divine energy that knows no limits. You become a dynamo all on your own, unfettered from the aches, pains, and demands of your body and ego.

This is amazing! Awesome! I've felt this energy myself. You've described it in the right words.

It is not my words but the direct hand of God that is amazing at this stage of your life. When your soul is riveted on meaningful intentions, then God sheds his veil and rearranges, recreates your world of possibilities. God pumps you up with courage and clears your hurdles. As if by magic, the blind find eyes, the dumb a tongue. Go back to your first laughter presentation, when you were "shy, sheepish, shrinking, and stuttering," and God from up above put the right words into your mouth, guided you through the right moves…

These are not coincidences or miracles. When your heart is in the right place and your spirit is pure, a higher power, a pulsating energy takes over. An invisible and unstoppable force forges your way forward, removing your obstacles and nudging you in the right direction.

Oh my God! This is so captivating. It explains so many of my own real-life experiences.

If you bathe in this soothing elixir long enough, then you begin to experience a kind of Godliness. This is the culmination of the journey of the soul, when you discover God around you and within you.

And that brings me to your final fate. When God so visibly lends you a helping hand, you cannot escape his blinding aura. You enter a new field of experience: the realm of the Godly experience. You are unshackled from your body and its needs, insulated from its suffering and discomfort. You seem detached from the goings-on in the world and view it from up above as one blessed with the supreme wisdom of God. You become highly sensitive to even the slightest tremor of feeling around you—a ball of vibrant, pulsating energy, electrified by the miracle of creation.

I've felt this feeling in flashes. The sheer force of the euphoric vitality is impossible to put into words.

It starts with a feeling of compassion in your heart and soul. Your absorption into meaning is a step forward when you render devoted service to the world. Your ultimate reward is what I have just described: the experience of God. A bond with the boundless omniscience of the Creator. Enlightenment. This goes beyond the self-actualization of your Maslow pyramid into uncharted territory. You are blanketed in a great peace, vibrating with wonderment.

Now you can discover the God within you. You can now enjoy omnipotence over your body and mind. In your own way, you can merge with the Creator. And so, my dear, **your penultimate wish is to experience God.**

As I understand, finally, God and Godliness are what all souls aspire to. Is that God's will?

As your creator, God shows you how compassion and love will bring you closer to Him, onto His lap. He gives and forgives repeatedly. He presents to you a world of abundance to enjoy to your fullest. God did not create you as a slave to sag with servitude under His commands, or to punish you for being disobedient. God created you as a soul, to enter the world, drink in its attractions, bask in its abundance, and enrich yourself from its vast array of experiences.

This talk with you has been a great eye-opener for me, a wonderful journey of self-exploration. You had all the right answers to my questions and all the right questions to my answers.

Nothing is for real in this world, but is a perception of your own reality. One man's food is another man's poison, just as a leftover morsel of food is trash for the rich but heavenly for the starving. Your consciousness of your good fortune, your sensitivity to this world and to nature, defines who and what you are. This is your reality.

In your younger days, you're on autopilot with the act of survival—growing up, learning, yearning, and earning. But as you mature, you have the option to release and realize the thirst for meaning inside you. And meaning unfetters your pent-up energy to polish and purify your soul so you can come closer to God, to become one with Him.

When you look for purpose and pursue meaning in your life, that's God's gentle reminder to help you tap your hidden potential and reap your greatest glory.

> *"I believe in the eternal quest for meaning and that the goal is the maturity of understanding, a cosmic consciousness in which one becomes a part of all life in a feeling of oneness and wholeness."*
>
> —Sigurd F. Olson

And for me, this reminder came when my soul was stolen by spreading laughter. It's fascinating, the way our souls figure in God's creation.

Creation is God's ceaselessly unfolding drama. Nothing ever dies, just as nothing is ever born. Water douses fire, which in turn evaporates water. Both turn into air, which is now fire and now water.

Death is a part of life, and death is another birth in the life of a soul. You are now a participant in life and now its spectator. Ultimately, there is no superior and no inferior, no coming and no going. Your journey is never-ending.

And where do we fit into this scenario?

You are simply a field of energy that changes form—from physical matter to metaphysical matter. Your soul is now encased in a body, now vanishes into nothingness. It is all the while a pulsating presence, constantly conscious and alive, a seeker of God and Godliness.

What exactly do we feel when we've perceived God and Godliness?

You experience superconsciousness—a state of dynamic awareness. You may have sensed it during moments of inner calm. When you feel so highly sensitized to feeling and to sympathy, you develop a strong intuition. That is when you begin to merge with creation and the Creator.

Can you give me some advice or some tips on how I can become more soulful, more peaceful?

Tap into your **soular energy**.

CHAPTER 8

CONNECTING THE DOTS

 I've come a long way with you. We've discussed many interesting things. For some reason, I've emerged as a different person after our talk.

But we seem to have veered off the original course of our conversation. Don't get me wrong, but I don't see the clear connection with my concerns.

 The connection of the dots is almost done, and you'll soon see the full picture as it emerges. We can address all your concerns now.

 I talked about my impatience, frustration, bitterness, and inner anger, then my guilt and guile, self-doubt, and skepticism. You defined your identity, then pointed out our human features, faculties, and failings. What's the connection? What's the point you're leading up to?

 This point. It's the right moment to connect the dots. Because only now have you the right knowledge of who you are, what life and death is, what God is, and the connection between these mysteries.

It would have been premature for me to speak earlier, because only now do you know where your giving and meaning can lead to. You now know more about your strengths, weaknesses, and your infinite potential. Above all, you have a clearer awareness of the soul that lies in your heart and a route to the Godly experience.

I came to you because my soul was stolen by forces I did not understand. You're right—I now understand myself better.

All souls instinctively gravitate toward love, which is the most alluring force on the planet and God's master creation. You had no choice but to follow your soul and make your peace with it. As a soulless body, you would be an empty shell with no identity—just a useless parasite.

Even as I've embraced and espoused my soul, I continue to be discomfited with day-to-day disturbances, distressed by disorder, thrown off-balance by trivialities such as social mannerisms that stray out of the norm. I must confess that I'm yet haunted by habitual sarcasm and cynicism. I'm still suspicious and distrustful of others' intentions. And I indulge my bodily urges without restraint. Didn't you notice the fulsome folds of flab around my waist?

How can all of this coexist with my giving and my search for meaning in life?

Because you continue to have your human hungers?

Yes. It's why I sought you out in the first place. The act of spreading laughter enamored my dormant soul and opened up a whole new world for me, but I'm still tormented by my desires and weaknesses.

God made you as a biological organism with bodily needs. So what harm can there be in the zestful satisfaction of your physiological desires? When the Buddha persevered with penance, his body protested with hunger. Then the Great Buddha, too, realized that hunger needs food, and so he espoused the middle way as the right way.

It is pointless to harbor any guilt for satisfying your physiological wants, provided that you retain a sense of balance.

What's that?

Nature's built-in system of equilibrium. Both overeating and under-eating are problems. That also applies to sleep and exercise and other bodily needs: too much and too little both lead to problems.

Routine maintenance and care keeps your car reliable and durable, and that's the way it works with your body. Look after it. Your body is a vehicle to take you on the longest and most exciting adventure of your life, so respect it. Use it, don't abuse it. Adopt the middle way.

Hmm. That makes sense. I may be able to hold my bodily needs in balance, but that's not so easy with my emotions.

Your angers, worries, and frustrations are a product of your genetic evolution. All of you humans are victims of an inner conflict that you must resolve on your own. Remember what the old Cherokee Indian said.

So my inner turmoil is my own lookout? Here to stay?

On both counts, no—because there are ways to resolve these issues. What makes you specifically uncomfortable with yourself?

My reactive, judgmental nature; my attitude, my sarcasm; extreme emotions; dark images; and the ensuing guilt. These are not in harmony with the purer feelings I've recently experienced.

Your guilt comes from stoking negative feelings in you. Is it because you've committed what the religious rectors call "sins"?

What sins?

The sin of your sexual imagery is a good example. Your religions don't recognize your sexuality and spawn guilt in you, because that is what supports their existence.

The guilt I feel isn't entirely born out of disobedience to my religion. I wonder why you ridicule religion the way you do.

I'm against religion because it puts you on the wrong track of guilt. The right quality of guilt should be born out of your conscience, which alone should judge what is sinful and what isn't. Guilt is a choice, born of fear, and religion fuels that fear, such as the fear of "hell" for "being bad" by missing or disobeying your religious services and sermons.

Your holy books are often used as a hammer to make a point or win an argument, quoting the written word as superior to reason.

Come on, there's always a free choice to follow religion or not.

Thank God for this, though in medieval times you could be burned at the stake for speaking out this way. Even today many societies condemn defiance to their religion and deny social privileges to the outcasts.

That's your view, but to be honest I'm too glued to my religious grounding and owe a lot to it for reaching out to my soul.

My dear chap, you arrived where you did not by rote chanting your religious writings but by religiously following your conscience. You should liken religion to a banana skin, which you must forcibly touch and then unpeel to reach the actual fruit inside.

You mean religion is just the outer covering, not the actual fruit?

Absolutely. It's part of the journey, or one of the routes, but not the destination. The goal, the kernel or fruit inside, is God and Godliness. There's more love and purity in an hour of selfless social work than in ten hours of mindlessly chanting religious hymns.

That makes sense, I suppose.

Swami Vivekananda—the famous Indian seer and sage, said that "it is good to be born in a religion, but it is bad to die in a religion." Your religion is something to grow out of, because the true nature of spirituality can rise in you only when religion has ebbed in you. Indeed, where religion ends, spirituality begins.

Your view is too radical. I'll need time to let this sink in.

Take all the time you want. In the meantime, all religions thrive for their existence on goading you with guilt. Most devotees pay lip service and perform religious deeds to assuage the guilt of committing a long list of sins. And guilt, my dear, is born out of the fear of what may happen by offending the gods.

So the underlying emotion of my guilt is fear?

Unfortunately so. Whether or not this fear is fostered and fomented by religion, the sad truth is that **fear is what brings out your worst**.

Fear enters you as imagination and exits as reactions. There is the fear of being taken advantage of, the fear of failure, the fear of not having enough, of not being enough. You fear the worst for yourself and your loved ones, and worry.

You could be right, but are you sure that fear is the cause of all my problems?

Your instinctive reactions are a hangover of your animal origins. The law of the jungle forces you to fight, freeze, or flee if you can't face it. Your frustration, bitterness, and anger occur because you can't face and can't bear the actual outcomes that confront you. Think carefully and judge for yourself. Each of your prickly emotions is rooted in one fear or another.

I guess you're right, if you broaden the definition of fear. But are you sure that fear is our foremost reaction?

At least 90 percent of the time, as a knee-jerk response. That's the way you humans are hardwired. Fear is the primary source of your negative raw emotions, because the fight, freeze, or flee options manifest themselves as hostility, hate, hurt, horror, or scorn, vengeance, disgust, jealousy, despair, and worry. Fear may work its way through its lieutenant, guilt, by infusing you with shame, remorse, isolation, dejection, and humiliation. Often the fear of fear causes more harm than the fear itself, because you die a thousand deaths in anticipation of facing the one death.

So fear is the biggest cause of our unhappiness. How do you dispel it?

At this stage, I'm simply pinning down the root cause of your inner conflict and confusion. Your life is a constant battle of facing the monster of fear.

And aren't *you* this monster?

So I am. I am the largest dot to connect, the largest piece of your jigsaw puzzle. I, as the anti-God, am the trigger of your fear. And remember, I live

"Let me assert my firm belief that the only thing we have to fear is fear itself—nameless, unreasoning, unjustified terror which paralyzes needed efforts to convert retreat into advance."
—Franklin D. Roosevelt

right there in your heart, next to God. Both are felt, not touched or seen.

Fear is what you conjure, and you can give it any shape you want. It is the biggest illusion, the most real ghost that haunts you 24-7, both in broad daylight and through your dreams at night.

You make it sound as if we're masochists and the cause of our own suffering.

That's correct. You are the architect of your fear, since you give it shape and form.

Then it should be easy to rub off the building plans, or make new and good ones.

Not easy, but possible. And that is your biggest battle in life: an ongoing fight to curb and control the fear impulse and reactions within you. Remember that a while ago, I said that your greatest victory is the one over your inner self, not over forces external to you.

See how this talk makes sense now rather than earlier!

Is catering and pandering to the ego also driven by fear?

To a large extent. The fear that somebody's going to exceed you, defeat you. Ostentatious behavior is a prop to support the ego that is saying, "I have this, you don't." Take the prop away and the ego falls flat. That's another fear.

Is there an easy way to tame the fear monster inside us?

That's a separate topic. Since fear provokes your negative thoughts and emotions, and fear is an illusion, then so are your resultant emotions. Guilt is born of your illusory fear and is itself an illusion that saps your energy.

If it's any solace to you, I'll say that each and every human has negative thoughts and emotions that are unreal. You're no different.

So it's okay to feel angry and disturbed? To have weaknesses?

Sure. Your flaws and failings are petty; treat them as such and ignore them. They are simply the little idiosyncrasies that keep you human. If you dwell on them too much, you pour energy on your eccentricities. This will merely make them leap up to life, as fuel does to fire.

Try not to make a big deal of the fears that haunt you.

That's easier said than done!

Another common failing born of fear is your being judgmental of both others and yourself. To feel stronger and better about yourself, you look for weaknesses in your peers. You judge and condemn others with ease. And oh! You're staring at the floor so intently. Looking for ants?

Umm, your words just rang a bell…about my intolerance of others.

Equally devastating is how you judge yourself. When you have failed in some way, your confidence is shattered and your spirit is injured. Dark, delusional doubts surround you as you open the doors to disease. Your energy is sapped.

> *"If you judge people, you have no time to love them."*
> —Mother Theresa

Isn't that natural?

I repeat that your resilience is what counts. Your success in life is about how you handle your failures, how high you bounce when you hit bottom.

You've put some common human traits into simple words. This helps, but I'm not so sure that it will stop our fears.

Understanding yourself is critical to healing yourself. In the meantime, your impatience, irritability, and indignation are important stages in your growth. Your experience from these is constructive because it is a learning and maturation process, an essential step in the distillation of your soul.

Does this help to relieve your angst?

> *"We are each our own devil, and we make this world our hell."*
> —Oscar Wilde

I'm feeling more comfortable with myself, now that I can see my negativity as part of the larger picture.

The devil—that's me—is always trying to win your attention. As with your bodily desires, your mental and emotional provocations continue to growl for nourishment. People and events around you will continue to insult and irk you. Your first reaction is the animalistic fight response, brought on by your impatience and indignation. Becoming more soul conscious is the only way to subdue and surpass your impatience and intolerance.

When you are in the purer energy flow and glow of soul-consciousness, your ego is automatically suppressed. This happens almost by stealth, and your negative reactionary impulses are checked and contained.

In your own words a while ago, when you grow soulfully, "it brings a great relief from clutter and confusion…"

Just as light dispels darkness, so do love and courage conquer hate and fear. I will soon talk about how you can mask your fears with courage, and your darkness with the sunshine of the soul.

Indeed, soul-consciousness is a sobering, softening influence on the hard, harsh impulses of negativity. Do you think that I harbor my inner confusion because of a poorly developed soul-consciousness?

The uplifting emotions from your giving have healed your wounded spirit to a large extent. You will continue to rise above these irritants as you pursue soul-consciousness.

In the weighing scale of fear versus courage, your fear-driven feelings sometimes sit heavier than your courageous, giving, and soulful side. When the scales are tipped in favor of the fight, freeze, or flight syndrome, then negative emotions take over.

On the other hand, courage trumps fear. So your life journey is about how to build up the amount of courage and compassion on your weighing scale so as to tip it in your favor. A great turning point comes when your priorities

> *"Why should we love our enemies? The first reason is fairly obvious. Returning hate for hate multiplies hate, adding deeper darkness to a night already devoid of stars. Darkness cannot drive out darkness; only light can do that. Hate cannot drive out hate; only love can do that."*
>
> —Martin Luther King, Jr.

are switched.

I'm confident that as you continue to mature, the little pinpricks you've highlighted will pester and provoke you less and less. When your soul becomes your best friend, you're up above, and everything down below is small and secondary.

I'm a bit overwhelmed by the simplicity of your words. You've certainly connected the dots and completed the picture of my situation. And you're right; I find your logic easier to understand now that you've lifted the veil on the mysteries of life. I especially liked your description of the human condition.

The one thing I like in the nature of the beast is your remarkable ability to rise above your lower nature. If you really set your mind to it, nothing can match you humans for sheer determination and endurance, with an ingenuity to match.

My mind is full of thoughts all the time, racing here and there, turning and churning all the time. Is that normal?

The average human mind is home to around sixty thousand thoughts each day, mostly born of emotional blips. This is why it is important to feel good feelings, because that is what will tame and mellow your wild imagination.

Wow! I'm relieved that I'm as normal as anybody and my condition isn't too bad.

But your report card is. Here it is:

You're a tough taskmaster, hard to please.

Self-knowledge	:	Vague and incomplete
Ego & Pride	:	Dangerously high
Internal fears	:	High
Gravity of your condition	:	Low
Resilience, will to improve	:	Half-Decent
Outlook	:	Excellent

Mind

Body

Spirit

Soul

Harmony

Joy

Love

Peace

Hope

Truth

You cornered me into presenting only the view that ran counter to yours. That in itself was shortsighted. Then you spoke in a verbose fashion, airing your views, thinking you're the cat's whiskers.

Is that how I sounded?

Professorial. Smug and know-it-all. Your understanding isn't bad, but crude, broken, incomplete. You could not comprehend the depth of your emotions or where to place them. You failed to appreciate the potential of your discoveries from giving and finding meaning. And you were clueless as to the final direction and destination of your life.

I must concede that I've learned a great deal from your wisdom. You've shed light on a lot of my misconceptions. I now look forward to getting some practical advice from you on how to elevate myself spiritually.

Just follow the dictates of your soul, and you'll be fine.

CHAPTER 9

A TALK ON THE WALK

🙏 I feel lighter after what you've said. I'm hoping now for some pointers on how to walk the talk.

🔱 I have merely described creation for what it is. Anyway, what pointers do you want? Where shall we start?

🙏 From the beginning.

🔱 As a beginning, you've got to recognize my existence—the anti-God—equally as you do the existence of God. To learn to accept me, humor me, befriend me, tame me.

🙏 A long time ago, I used to be a smoker. To kick the habit, I attended group therapy where it was suggested that over the years I had created a nicotine monster inside my stomach. The monster could be kept at bay only with a steady, regular diet. If this diet was delayed or denied, he would thrash around like a hungry crocodile, demanding its food, its fix.

🔱 Ha-ha! You certainly know how to flatter me! I admire the articulate manner in which you've portrayed me. You'll make a good artist.

That's who I am, the monster that lives inside you. Feed him and you make him stronger, starve him and you pare his power over you.

Keep him on a leash, and you'll be fine. Occasionally the monster will howl and cut loose, and the way to rein him in is to turn a deaf ear to his wails and cries. Stay calm and composed as you reckon with his ruckus.

That's good advice, though I don't know how easy it is to follow all the time.

A good idea is to paste the feeling of love and laughter right over the monster's face. It's a skill you can easily learn.

So much for the monster. Surely you have something more to say?

Ultimately, your salvation lies in awakening your soul-consciousness. The method to achieve this is to open up your sensitivity to the suffering of others and do your bit, however small, for other souls in need of understanding and comfort.

There is no other purpose to your existence, other than for you to find this purpose. The only meaning of your life is to discover this meaning. When you offer your healing touch to others, you actually heal yourself in the purest, most effective way.

So my best advice is for you to embrace compassion. Make a passion out of compassion. Become religiously compassionate.

Religiously? I thought that you hated the word.

The religious regime is one of my pet peeves, not the act of practicing it. You must exercise compassion religiously, with total commitment and devotion. When you are compassionate, you raise the antenna of your sensitivity. You not only sense the suffering of others but also the fullness of your own world.

And when you appreciate the great abundance that God has bestowed on you, then from this higher plane your own problems seem small compared to those of others. This excites a feeling of gratitude in you, along with appreciation of your lot in life.

This is when you enter a positive field of energy, of love—connected to God and His life-giving radiance.

You're right. Compassion does open up the door to self-discovery.

And to reach God. God is pure love, the force that helps you bring out your best through your positive good side. Compassion will help you to expand your consciousness. It works through continually recognizing, respecting, refining, and renewing your conscience. The feeling of sympathy, of being sensitive to the needs of others and your world, is the underlying emotion behind compassion. Amongst the vehicles to exercise compassion are your giving and your search for meaning.

How exactly does compassion work?

In science-speak, you have what are called mirror neurons in your cognitive system. Located in the brain's motor cortex, the cells fire in sympathy with what you see. When someone smiles, these cells replicate the response and you actually feel the same feeling yourself. A look of panic on somebody's face invokes a quick, heart-wrenching concern in your own self before questioning the source and nature of the panic. When people are sympathetic toward you, then your own response is reciprocal—full of caring and sharing.

When your sensitivity is heightened to perceive the suffering around you, your empathetic response is strongly fired up, and you respond with giving, helping, healing.

My own act of getting people to laugh was perhaps grounded in compassion too, as an urge to heal. I found this to be meaningful.

Surely you have some more tips on how to build up soul-consciousness.

Aha! Amongst the thousands of *To Do* lists, you want another neat course outline to mechanically follow.

That would make life easier!

Your best learning in life is experiential. You must live through your disappointments to learn from them, grow from them. It is only from this chiseling and polishing that your soul will shine through. The way of God is to flower from free choice, not a book of rules.

Then how about a tiny booklet?

What do you want, a *Guide to the Soul 101*?

Oh, never mind. Would you amplify a bit on the nature of compassion?

> *"If you want others to be happy, practice compassion. If you want to be happy, practice compassion."*
> —Dalai Lama

Compassion is a frame of mind, an attitude that is felt. Once you exercise compassion, you blank out the world of your own gripes and groans, and replace it with the thought and feeling of caring. You can be compassionate toward other people, toward animals, toward nature. It is equally important to be compassionate toward yourself and treat your own soul with kindness.

Can you be a bit more specific? How do you become more compassionate?

Through empathy. You must develop the ability to put yourself in others' shoes, in others' hearts, and feel their joys, their hopes, their woes.

Close your eyes and transport yourself into the world of others. As you dwell on this thought, you can summon this feeling. The world is now visible through special tinted spectacles called compassion. Now try to view the people in your life, groups, animals, and nature around you in a new, sympathetic light. Witness, then get into, the hearts of those around you. Feel their pain and suffering. Experience their emotions as they battle with life's pressures. Equally, feel it when they rejoice in their happier moments.

Feel connected with nature and your place in it. Extend your appreciation, sympathy, and compassion to plants and animals too.

It's a simple exercise that will open up your heart to empathy—the first step toward compassion. New feelings will emerge in your heart. The sympathy that will arise will put your own annoyances and grievances into the background. The doubts and fears that live in your heart will evaporate, and you will experience a new lightness within you—a great peace. A feeling of calmness and reconciliation will replace your own inner turmoil.

Compassion is the trigger to the warm glow you spoke of and will change your outlook and attitude, unlock a new you. It will liberate your soul to rise and reach out for higher fulfillment.

Not all of us can find suitable outlets to exercise compassion.

There you are wrong. Compassion begins as a state of mind, of being aware and alive to the world and its needs. Are you respecting the feelings and rights of others? Is your heart full of consideration and a smile to reach out to others in need?

Compassion does not extend only to other humans but to the world at large. Do you value or waste the resources of plant and animal life, water and energy? Is your consumption based on need or greed? Do you use or abuse God's gifts by encouraging nature to flower and prosper, or are you an agent of its death and destruction?

I'm not sure I understand.

You must become sensitive to the earth, which is wailing and wilting under the ravages you subject it to. You can maybe afford the expense, but do you really need to burn more fuel than necessary, use more food and water than necessary? Do you recycle the plastics with care? Are you a parasite on this world, depleting and contaminating its resources, or are you an ally of God to add to nature's bounty? This part of your conscience will awaken when your sense of ethics joins hands with your conscience and compassion.

Oh my God! There seem to be no horizons to the reach of compassion.

Compassion is a voluntary feeling out of free choice. When your sense of compassion is developed, you have surpassed the myopic, materialistic view of life and graduated to a spiritual one.

> "The word philanthropy has its roots in the Greek language meaning 'love for mankind.' It was never meant to apply only to donors of thousands or millions of dollars."
>
> —Arthur Frantzreb

Compassion is not a monopoly of Bill Gates and Warren Buffet but a blazing torch that they hold high so that others can see the path. You can donate your time to a worthy individual, a worthy organization, a worthy cause. Volunteer work is one of the easiest and purest ways to give. You can appreciate and lend a hand to raise those who need a leg up—the lonely and depressed, the ill or those born into less fortunate circumstances than you.

Education is the one investment that does not succumb to the law of diminishing returns. It can expand the horizons of the less fortunate and raise the quality of their lives. Education for the destitute is a surer way of securing their future life than direct charity.

The opportunities to give surround each and every one of you. Give of your time, your money, your energy, above all your love, but give. Even in the smallest of your giving will heaven rain down to touch and comfort your soul. Giving offers a meaning to your life.

Aha! So all that I was praising—the giving, purpose, and meaning—come alive because of compassion. Do speak on.

Initially, you will feel compassionate in fits and starts. Try to focus on this as a way of life. If your mind wavers and wanders, rivet yourself back to feeling compassionate, whatever your subject or object. Let the heart glow and flow, let it become alive and aware to the world. Over a period of time, when you've tasted and felt the warmth of new sensations, it will become your automatic response and reaction.

Compassion is an exercise in raising the level of your sensitivity, of deepening the depth of your heart to both laugh and cry in a fuller, more intense manner. This opens up your creativity, intuition, and insight into your higher self. Compassion will unfetter you from your attachments, pinings, and pangs and open up a new world where only love exists. You will heal your spirit and re-energize your soul. When you have learned this exercise, you will be released from fear's grip and a great transformation will come over you.

Learn and develop your own unique technique for entering a compassionate world, and you will witness firsthand the change in yourself.

I'm not so sure it's easy to turn on the feeling at will so effortlessly, but it's certainly worth trying.

Your heart will light up as never before. Your yogis and seers have learned through meditation the method of switching off their negative emotions and masking these with positive, cosmic energy. That is compassion at work.

You may be puzzled, but the intensity of the experience will bring you back for more, as you discover the purpose of your life.

Look at your own self: you chose to give to the world by making people laugh. The starfish boy did it his own way. Even in the smallest act of kindness there is a connection to the divine. Through kindness and consideration, you open up new avenues of feeling, new vistas of spiritual growth. It is the ultimate perennial joy known to man, and leads to bliss.

I was lucky to have discovered laughteryoga, which captivated my soul, but not all of us can be so fortunate. Can you suggest some easy ways for how each of us can find a meaningful activity in life?

Your meaning is not what you pluck off a tree, or buy into. It is your own unique drawing—your exclusive creation. One man's meaning is another man's malice.

The meaning of meaning is a personal, prized feeling, a privately felt glow that fires you up from within. It is your nature to value most what you learn yourself, earn yourself. When you attach meaning to what you do, it becomes the most powerful motivator of your life. And so, for it to work, perforce it must be your own brainchild, your own creation.

Not all of us are blessed with creativity. But I guess it's for each of us to try, to find our personal compass. I'm lucky to have found mine, and the joyous sensations it brings. But please, Mr. D—life can't be all giving, sharing, and purpose. You've got to make ends meet too.

> *"The best way to find yourself is to lose yourself in the service of others."*
> —Gandhi

Sure. Go about your chores, fulfill your family and social objectives, bask in the world's delights. Play. Play some more. Live life to the full, zestfully. Earn a fortune, but give back—generously—to a single person, to nature, to humanity, or to a cause that benefits the world. Give in your own unique way. This is what will keep you human and alive, and keep your inner monster locked up. In your own words, giving is actually getting.

You mean even selfishly oriented giving is okay?

Giving as a financial investment doesn't work because it fails to produce the warm glow effect. True giving is without an agenda, without motives of social, financial, or political dividends. Only in selfless giving do you reap the best spiritual enrichment and healing from your giving. When it is impossible for the giver to dissociate him or herself from the social rewards, humility helps.

From the way you've described your spiritual staircase, to take a stride up you've got to devote your life to spiritual pursuits. Some of us can be fired up for this, but for many it's a tough prescription with all of life's demands.

On the contrary, nothing could be easier. In the pursuit of spiritual meaning, God has built higher emotional rewards exceeding the lower-order sensory thrills and ego kicks. The research I quoted endorsed this finding. Thousands of respondents confirmed that the most rewarding happiness-inducing activity they experienced was in "engaging leisure and spiritual activities."

The engaging activities are those that require you to stretch your skills, battle the odds, and win, and spirituality is drawn from the foundation of compassion.

God helps you discover your bottomless pools of strength, hidden energy, and talents when you find a purpose. Remember what you said about discovering meaning: "It doesn't matter how lofty your purpose or how humble your actual achievements toward this purpose. What matters is that you become energized the moment you begin chipping away toward it…"

Yes, I remember now. And I'm already feeling light, enthusiastic, and energized.

There's more to it. God doesn't stop at helping you find your hidden strengths. Once your intent is on track and detached from the outcome, God takes over and opens up a whole new world of possibilities and opportunities for you. When you are ready to give to the world, His omnipotence works to remove your obstacles and smooth your way.

Was it not so in your own case? Go back to your nervousness at the start of your laughter sessions, when your timid and trembling temperament found a new confidence at the right moment.

That's so true. It's as if God put the words into my mouth. God removed my apprehensions when I was ready to act.

When your awareness is heightened, when your consciousness is enhanced, you see light where previously you saw darkness. Think of yourself as a field of energy living as a miniscule derivative of, and inside a larger energy field. That is God. Like a star in the galaxy. When you are plugged into the cosmic power of God, you draw from His infinite energy and with this you can achieve anything that you set your mind to.

In so many little ways, God is helping and encouraging you to ride over your hurdles, so that you can taste and enjoy the greatest bliss that the world has to offer. This is the nature of self-realization and self-actualization, when your own energy has merged with God's. It is a union with God.

And that, my dear, is the Godly experience I spoke of.

I can see how willfully practicing compassion will smooth the way into giving and finding meaning. Don't you have some simpler one-two-three steps?

You need a formula, don't you? To memorize and mindlessly manage? You want a do-it-yourself list of dos and don'ts to add to an already crowded schedule. You want a chart to look at, a tape or a book. You want a toy to put into your pocket for the answers.

Reminders always help. But I'll understand if there are no gadgets and gimmicks.

The answers are in your heart where God lives, within yourself. Everything I've said is about feeling, which you will experience once you exercise compassion. You will heighten your sensitivity to the wailing world around you. You will feel its pain when it is wounded and exult when courage trumps fear.

Once compassionate feelings have wormed their way into your heart, you will modify and moderate your attitude. You will be a changed person, alive to the world not just sometimes but all the time.

This state of blissful ecstasy will keep you from turning back to your previous empty existence, however pleasure-soaked it may have been.

In my own case, the laughter activity stole my soul and opened up a whole new world of feelings. Sometimes, I still can't believe what hit me, but I'm a changed person. How and why this came to be still puzzles me.

I'll repeat two small observations here, which you can treat as advice. The first is how compassion and giving are related to abundance. When you presuppose abundance in your world, you are feeling grateful for your good fortune, and this instantly lights up your heart from within.

The second point is how compassionate giving is detached from the outcome, and you become a truly free spirit.

We've discussed this earlier, and I'm beginning to appreciate it now. Surely there are more ways to point us toward soul-consciousness.

Sure, but I'm not so sure you'll understand.

Try me! My perception and sensitivity nodes are wide awake.

You are a field of energy—pounding, pulsating, throbbing. You pick up signals from the environment around you and emit signals into it.

What do you mean?

Didn't we discuss how you need to give love to get love, give a smile to get a smile, give healing to get healed? The mirror neurons that force your feelings to mirror what you see in others?

We did, and on the face of it I agree that yes, you're right. But how does this give and take actually work? What is this exchange?

The famous physicist Newton's third law of motion: "**to every action there is an equal and opposite reaction.**"

This applies not only to physics but also to metaphysics. You beam a feeling into the universe, and the universe beams it right back to you.

This sounds too far-fetched.

I'll reemphasize that you are a vibrant field of energy, with an antenna to both receive signals from the universe and transmit your signals back to it. Feelings are the language of the soul. Tell me, how do you think feelings are communicated?

I suppose you simply tell the other person how you feel.

Hmm. I did say you wouldn't understand. My dear chap, the passing on of feelings is 50 percent body language, 40 percent tone, and only 10 percent words.

You've got to be joking! Our language is expressive and developed.

And so it is. Language is a useful tool to communicate information and knowledge. But feelings are only 10 percent passed on with words.

That's amazing! And how does this connect to what you said about us being fields of energy?

When two souls are on the same wavelength of feelings, no words are necessary for communication and they simply radiate how they feel toward each other. Elevated souls emit an aura of peace. When you enter their presence, you cannot but share in their inner calm and compassion.

You're right! I remember long ago as a kid I was part of an audience with the Dalai Lama, and I could actually sense his great positive energy.

Great, evolved souls generate powerful cosmic waves of love and peace. But even for everyday souls, most feelings are communicated nonverbally.

You mean by telepathy?

In a manner of speaking. It's the same way that animals sense the way you're feeling. A dog will either bark at you or wag his tail, depending on whether you emit waves of fear or love.

That's so true! I've personally felt it hundreds of times.

Your feelings work like a mirror. Fear in others incites fear in yourself. Resentment directed at you provokes resentment in you. If you are attacked verbally or otherwise, then your first reaction is to retaliate in the same way. An act of kindness toward you makes your heart well up with kindness toward others.

Mirror mirror on the wall

The good you seek in others, is your good quality too
The faults you find in others, are your faults as well
Anger towards others provokes their anger towards you
The beauty you see around you, is your beauty
The hope you see in others, is your best hope

Seek to understand, and you will be understood
Listen, and you will be heard
Shout, and you'll be shouted at
Blame, and you will be blamed
Hate, and you will be hated

Care for, and you'll be cared for
Give to others, and you'll be given to
Thank, and you will be thanked
Praise, and you will be praised
Love, and you will be loved

To change your world, change yourself
You can get rich only by enriching others
Smile at the world, and it will smile back at you
Your world is a mirror that reflects your attitude to it,
Give your best to the world, and it'll give its best back to you.

You mean the same reaction will reflect back to each and every action of ours?

Absolutely. Your feelings can be from one of two groups. One is the fear group, which provokes anger, shame, jealousy, sorrow, cynicism, self-doubt, and all the other negative emotions and sub-emotions that go with it. The other is the love group of peace, hope, serenity, community, kindness, courage, compassion, and zest. A fear-oriented emotion gets a fear-oriented emotion thrown back at it, and it works the same for love.

> *"Everyone has two choices. We're either full of love ... or full of fear."*
> —Albert Einstein

How does it work? What are the nuts and bolts of this?

Like energy seeks out and conjoins with like energy. Anger directed at you incites your own anger. If you are surrounded by skeptical and suspicious people, then so will you become.

On the other hand, if others respect you and your wishes, then you have no choice but to respect them in return. Didn't I talk a while ago about how you must give love to get love, give respect to get respect, give a smile to get a smile?

And so you did, but what are you driving at?

Just that **you must choose to swim in the right energy pool**, because you'll always attract more of the energy you harbor inside you. The world will manifest before your eyes what your mind and heart is focused on. It will create the situations that correspond to your thoughts and beliefs.

I like that. Can you talk some more about this?

If you're feeling angry, then this is what you radiate toward the world, and this is exactly what the world reflects back at you. Cynics hang out with cynics. If you always fear the worst, suspect bad intentions in others, and habitually complain, then for sure your wait will be well rewarded with negative outcomes in your life. You'll have plenty to suspect and plenty to complain about. Your reality as it unfolds is always in sync with your soular energy.

How?

Your body language and tone are the most powerful tools to pass on feelings—the expression of the soul. If you radiate sympathy, then this is how others will feel toward you. All the positive emotions of love, peace, joy, courage, kindness, and compassion act as a powerful antenna to attract and direct positive energy toward you, and also shape positive situations for you. This positive energy will encourage your courage, empower your power, add enjoyment to your joy.

> *"To rejoice in another's prosperity, is to give content to your own lot: to mitigate another's grief, is to alleviate or dispel your own."*
> —Thomas Edwards

Vice versa, if you swim in the fear pool of energy, you coexist with anger, self-doubt, shame, jealousy, and intolerance. First, the good energy people will sense your bad vibes and avoid you. Second, the world will manifest negative outcomes toward you, and you'll continue to wallow in this quicksand.

Can you give some examples?

In a social or work situation, you learn of somebody's outstanding success. If you give a dour and disinterested look, then people with good vibes will shrink away from you. When positive energy deserts you, so does courage, confidence, and cooperation. This practically guarantees that nobody will come forward to lend you a hand or a leg up.

If you're looking at a wealthy and successful person with averted eyes and envy, then these are the signals the universe picks up. You'll be shut out of the company of positive people or positive situations that may help you become wealthy too.

It's simple. Your feelings are your posture toward the world. You think your feelings are private, but in reality the people around you and the universe pick up your emotions so very easily. An angry spouse may act civil, but his or her partner is bound to sense the bug immediately.

The same logic extends to the universe at large. Loving, compassionate people are treated lovingly and compassionately. Angry and disgruntled ones will have plenty to be disgruntled about because this is the energy others will beam back toward them.

If you're focused on problems, you'll find an ample supply of problematic situations. And if you're looking for solutions, you'll be well rewarded too. The positive people see an opportunity in every problem and attack problems with energy and zest. The negative people see a problem in every opportunity and shy away and lose out—the more so for lack of even trying. And failures are the food of cynicism.

I guess there *is* some truth in what you're saying, because I've experienced being dragged down by negative people many times. I suppose it's because our feelings define our identity, and these feelings are so vulnerable, so fragile. Even if our feelings are communicated nonverbally, why do they fall prey to those of others?

Every one of you, consciously or unconsciously, affects the objects and people around you—including yourselves—on a continual basis. You call yourself a "Laughter Therapist," don't you? Then you should know that the key to your success is that laughter is intrinsically contagious. So it is with emotions, which are equally contagious. All emotions float around as an electrical charge that passes from one body to another, from one object to another. No words are exchanged. The energy field of one heart touches and eclipses the energy field of another and bingo!—the two merge.

> "When you choose to be pleasant and positive in the way you treat others, you have also chosen, in most cases, how you are going to be treated by others."
> —Zig Ziglar

This is why you must be careful to stay in the right energy pool. One is a quicksand that pulls you down to the depths of despair; the other is a nourishing nectar that heals and elevates you.

It's fascinating! Emotions are unseen to the eye, but they rule our lives completely!

We are talking about soul-consciousness and soular energy. These color and shape all your emotions, all your feelings. A pure soul is one that does not stifle its conscience and is therefore clean, pure, loving, and giving. This is what it reflects to the world through its posture and its demeanor, and this is what the world beams back to it.

Vice versa, a guilty, troubled, and stressed soul exudes a body language and tone that is a dead giveaway to its underlying negativity.

When you're envious, your furtive glances and lack of warmth are sensed by others around you. This is how people will view you and how the world will relate to you. The energy you kick up into the air, whether born of love or born of fear, is the energy that will bathe you in real-life relationships and outcomes.

> *"If people around you aren't going anywhere, if their dreams are no bigger than hanging out on the corner, or if they're dragging you down, get rid of them. Negative people can sap your energy so fast, and they can take your dreams from you, too."*
>
> —Earvin Johnson

Many overly skeptical people look upon the world with a distorted, delusional, dark doubt. They will close their eyes to a world of opportunities, but lie in wait for the predator to pounce on them, even as their hair turns from gray to white. When in some convoluted way their prayers are answered and something "unfair" happens to them, their underlying doubts and negative beliefs are reinforced.

I see it! I know a lot of people like that! Just the other day, a friend remarked that "people who are bored *are* bores!"

Ha-ha! That's a good one, and very apt. The cynical, skeptical types are disinterested, oblivious to the wonders and opportunities of life. Such people find little to occupy them other than their complaints. So they're bored. And lo and behold—their company is boring too.

During your everyday life, you'll meet lots of people who talk endlessly about their aches and pains. This is their energy pool, and the universe will bring them a never-ending supply of further aches and pains.

You'll also meet people who love to complain—about the weather, about the high taxes, about their ill health, their political leaders, their generation, their workmates, their children, their spouses. Well, God will ensure that these people never run out of complaints! If something goes wrong, many will turn to blame rather than constructive reasoning. Welcome to Newton's law of motion! Blame and you will be blamed in return.

Anger begets plenty to get angry about. Jealousy and hatred are real killers—you direct the poison at somebody else, but you die as a result.

Do positive feelings evoke equally powerful positive outcomes?

Absolutely. And this is the essence of my talk with you. Be nice to people and the world. In return, people and the world will be nice to you. Rejoice in a feeling of nature's abundance, and nature will then actually grant you the abundance to rejoice about. Give freely and you'll get freely. If you're supportive and encouraging to others, this is what others will beam back towards you. Your attitude determines your altitude in life. So I'll say it again: you must swim in the right energy pool.

You can't escape Newton's law, which guarantees that your action energy comes back to you as reaction energy. Positive to positive, negative to negative. Throw up good intentions and good deeds in the air and in some indirect way the benefits will shower down back upon you. Emit bad signals into the universe and the universe will duly reward you with bad outcomes.

What's the guarantee that you'll always reap the rewards for being good?

How linear your thinking is—one-dimensional, confined to a neat little box. You want a one-hundred-dollar investment to be paid back by the same person, and with interest.

Your actions are almost never rewarded on a one-one-basis or in the same currency. The compensation for your good intent may be something unrelated, or simply your peace of mind. This by inference helps you take the right steps in life, which will end up more rewarding because of your positive attitude.

Bask and bathe in the warm glow you're familiar with when you touch your soul. Stay in this glow—in its radiance—and see how this mirrors good things for your mental and physical health: harmony with your surroundings, a great sense of community, a euphoric state of being alive and connected. Do you wish to put a price tag on this?

The law of cause and effect applies conversely to retribution as well. The Eastern Vedic law of karma says that the actions you take today may hold rewards or penalties for you in a different incarnation on earth. I'll make it simpler: even in this lifetime, your good or bad deeds aren't rewarded on a one-on-one basis, but on a universal basis.

How does it work, exactly?

Suppose a Mr. X has cheated and robbed you. You want to bash his head in and throw him behind bars, but he's disappeared. Alas, Mr. X will duly get his just punishment, but not by your hand, and maybe without your knowing it. The punishment may not be prison, but a lonely, loveless life on the run, an accident, ill health, nightmares, inner torment—whatever. Such punishment could be meted out by a third, unknown Mr. Y or by nature, by the elements. The splash of hurt created by Mr. X ripples back to him in an unseen manner, by an unseen hand.

As for your own suffering, you're either fulfilling your past life karma, or paying the price for having hurt a third Mr. Z in some unrelated way.

That's interesting. Personally I'd rather settle my scores myself, but if this is God's way, then so be it!

Here's a warning I must give you. If you're in the score-settling mode, then this by itself is the wrong energy field, which will sap your sanity. You must make a conscious decision to avoid the urge to punish, to fix, to retaliate. Leave this to God's will and wiles.

> *"Whatever is expressed is impressed. Whatever you say to yourself, with emotion, generates thoughts, ideas and behaviors consistent with those words."*
>
> —Brian Tracy

That isn't easy!

Your media says that revenge is a dish best served cold, but this is a feeling you must suppress. Whichever way you look at it, the feeling of revenge is poisonous. So please, fight the urge when it hits you. Fight it head-on.

Positive energy is like water to a raging fire. Douse, douse, douse.

I guess it's worth a try.

Your outside world is but a reflection of your inner self. It is your reality as you have created it—ominously oppressive for the diehard pessimists, and full of love, happiness, and joy for the optimists.

Every day, every hour, every minute, you are creating the causes that determine your effect, whether good or evil. The energy you project into the world decides how the world is perceived by your eyes, ears, nose, touch, and taste. Negative forces within you will produce negative effects, and vice versa.

If you believe that you are worth little, then you will actually receive little, because others see in you what you see in yourself. You are a product of your thoughts, the energy you let loose into the universe. Stay in the energy pool of goodness, giving, and greatness, and the universe will reflect this right back at you. Think doubt and fail—think victory and win. This is precisely why the wise advise you to make mentors of good people, because even their positive aura will serve to recharge and revitalize your positive energy field.

Aha! So if you initiate or beam some energy it goes into some sort of universal energy exchange. Then what comes back to you may be in a different time, a different currency, from a different source. Help and you'll be helped. Love and you'll be loved. Be positive, stay in a positive flow of energy, and the world will return this good energy in different ways.

You have it! Energy never dies; it simply changes form. The natural law of the universe will ensure that it ripples right back to you in some way.

Your thoughts and beliefs spill out of your every pore as feelings, as an attitude, whether you know it or not. The energy that you attract complements the energy you emit into this world.

Give to and you'll be given to. The presupposition behind giving is a feeling of abundance to give from. Keep this feeling alive and well. Bask in nature's abundance, in the abundance of your heart to open out

> *"Life is an echo—what you send out comes back."*
> —Anonymous

to as many as possible. You'll be surprised at the love and appreciation that's reflected back at you.

The flip side of this is fear, the feeling of not having enough, of not being enough. Fear is negative energy. This is the feeling of insufficiency and inadequacy, and your attitude to the world will ensure this insufficiency and inadequacy for you. What you'll lure are like-minded people who also live in fear, scantiness, and shortage. You'll repel people who could help you.

I can see the wisdom of what you're saying, but come on. You can't stay positive and peaceful at all times. Life is full of challenges, and there's plenty to get angry about, plenty to worry about, lots of stress.

Precisely why you must choose to swim in the right energy pool.

Angry? The monster's here. Time to chain him up. Depressed and oppressed? Aggressively suppress. Insulted? Breathe in, breathe out. Brush it off as somebody's negativity. Refuse to let it overpower you. Disappointed? It happens—don't let it ruin your day. The important thing is not to let failures haunt you, just as it's not a positive person's style to haunt or nag others for their failures.

That's easier said than done, sir! You can't just snap your fingers and—poof!— your problems have vanished.

At the start of our conversation, you complained of being cynical, withdrawn, and full of self-doubt. Is that not so?

So I did.

That's the wrong force to have within you. Make the switch to the correct energy pool. Keep your hopes and optimism alive. Even if your chances for victory are dim, proceed with zeal, a potent fervor. People will instinctively encourage the underdog. They will cheer for the enthusiastic one, not the certain victor. If you are enthusiastic, you will draw the energy from your audience better.

I suppose you're right there. But how do you handle bad luck? When the best of intentions are squashed by natural forces? That's so unfair and depressing.

My dear chap, bad things happen to good people with the same frequency that good things happen to bad people. The only difference is that the negative people don't grasp and appreciate the good things; instead, they magnify and aggrandize the bad things and add energy and life to these mishaps. The positive people fare better because while they rejoice and rejuvenate through the good things, they don't hang on to the disappointments of bad things. They've learned the very important skill of shrugging off their ill luck. They've discovered the secret of swimming in the right energy pool.

How can you jump over from one energy pool to another?

Life is not about being blessed with good things all the time and then performing the worst of wanton waste with these good gifts. Quite the converse is true. The true living of life is when, in spite of being exposed to the worst things, you make the best out of this bad situation.

> *"Life consists not in holding good cards but in playing those you hold well."*
> —Josh Billings

You mean there's no smooth sailing for anybody? That all lives come with both ups and downs?

Yes. And this is something you'd better get used to. We talked at length to describe the nature of the beast, which shows that even as you are irked by problems, your best moments are felt in overcoming them. So it is with feelings. Your compassion is ignited only by witnessing sorrow, others' or yours. This is the only way to touch your soul, to enter a new field of consciousness.

And I'm the head of the Sorrow Department. See the connection?

You did say that continuous elation is possible only through satisfying the soul.

Sensory gratification is never continuing. We discussed that. The only lasting gratification is through soul-consciousness. And only compassion will get you there, which is fired by sorrow. A human needs heartache to make him humane.

That's a glum prospect.

But it's the truth. And my advice is to befriend your disappointments and distress with the same ease as you welcome your achievements. Despair is as vital to you as your triumphs. Both are subject to the axiom "this, too, shall pass." And if you need to cope with discomfort, just swim over to the right energy pool.

That's a tall order! Life's not so simple!

This is a skill, a technique that your great people discovered and lived by. It's the ability to muzzle the cry of the little monster inside you before he overpowers you.

When you're assaulted by a disappointment or fear or circumstances that try your patience and your strength, then your trained intuition will tell you that the danger of negativity is knocking. You have to stop this fire dead in its tracks. Pour a generous helping of positive energy on the flames right away to put them out.

How?

Take charge of your thoughts, beliefs, and feelings. Change the channel that's bothering you and tune in to a good, soothing frequency. Recall and relive good feelings from happy memories. Willfully command yourself to dwell on positive feelings, to overwrite good thoughts on negative impulses. The two will overlap on your brain for a short while, but you'll soon develop the ability to override the negative moment.

Overwrite, overlap, override. Is it all that easy? You can't exactly store positive energy in a jug to pour onto problems.

You can. It's like pulling the right switch in your brain. Your animal reaction is to let the disappointment overwhelm and overtake you. That happens some 90 percent of the time to all of you.

You must train your reaction to first look for a moment of clarity. In this nanosecond when you see the sparks, you must reach out for your positivity jug. A fire extinguisher is kept handy for emergencies; so should you keep your jug of positivity fully topped up. Keep it handy to douse out the flames of negativity whenever they rise up.

What do you put into the jug?

Compassion toward others and the world, even if they have hurt you. Compassion toward yourself too, because this is what will nurse you back to your natural state of abundance and positivity.

The feeling of compassion is the key, the great river of which you keep some in your handy jug.

I did ask you about specific steps to take in order to feel compassionate at will. Like a quick switch-on. Is that possible?

> "*The stronger and greater your compassion, the stronger and greater your fearlessness and confidence.*"
> —Sogyal Rinpoche

You can spark the flow of compassion through some simple steps. These are the smaller streams that flow into the great river of compassion. Here I will speak of them, one by one:

"When you are grateful fear disappears and abundance appears."
—Anthony Robbins

"Be thankful for what you have; you'll end up having more. If you concentrate on what you don't have, you will never, ever have enough."

—Oprah Winfrey

"There is nothing that can have a more powerful effect on your mental health than the spirit of thankfulness."

—George E. Vandeman

"Gratitude is a vaccine, an antitoxin, and an antiseptic."

—John Henry Jowett

"Gratitude unlocks the fullness of life. It turns what we have into enough, and more. It turns denial into acceptance, chaos into order, confusion into clarity... It turns problems into gifts, failures into success, the unexpected into perfect timing, and mistakes into important events. Gratitude makes sense of our past, brings peace for today and creates a vision for tomorrow."

—Melodie Beattie

GRATITUDE

Gratitude is one of the most potent emotions you can exercise, to make an affirmation of your good fortune and the abundance that surrounds you. This is positive energy at its most powerful, and the aura will dispose your demeanor to give and receive good things from life.

Gratitude is triggered by compassion, and you already understand its presupposition of abundance, on which love flourishes. A large body of research suggests that grateful people have more energy, are less bothered by life's hassles, are more resilient in the face of stress, and enjoy better health. Grateful people suffer less depression than the rest of us and are generally more satisfied with life. Research shows that even others around grateful people noticed them as enjoying more energy, more optimism, and a better quality of life.

Each one of you has much to be grateful for, and that gratitude is due to individual persons, fate, events, organizations, God. The feeling of gratitude is a humble giving of thanks and evokes the same warm glow as outright physical giving. It deeply touches your soul and changes your persona to one filled with the gush of positive feelings. Gratitude is one of the most powerful emotions to awaken your soul and will act as a continuing motor to move you spiritually forward.

Never pass up an opportunity to be grateful, to God, to nature, to your family, to fate and fortune, to anybody or anything.

"Appreciation is a wonderful thing. It makes what is excellent in others belong to us as well."

—Voltaire

"There is more hunger for love and appreciation in this world than for bread."

—Mother Theresa

"If you wish your merit to be known, acknowledge that of other people."

—Anonymous

"One of the sanest, surest, and most generous joys of life comes from being happy over the good fortune of others."

—Archibald Rutledge

"Flatter me, and I may not believe you. Criticize me, and I may not like you. Ignore me, and I may not forgive you. Encourage me, and I may not forget you."

—William Arthur

"Note how good you feel after you have encouraged someone else…never miss the opportunity to give encouragement."

—George Adams

APPRECIATION

Appreciation is the act of expressing praise for another's goodness or positive traits. This lights up the heart in a similar way to gratitude. Psychologist Alice Isen, a Cornell University professor, has researched the good feelings generated by expressing appreciation. It releases the flow of dopamine to the brain, the chemical associated with happiness.

An admiration and cognizance of somebody else's efforts translates to an act of helping them, which makes them feel good too. The good feelings mirror right back to you and make you feel good. Many a marital conflict has been nipped in the bud by this simple tool, and you bask in a field of positive energy by appreciating, appreciating, and appreciating.

As human beings, you are hardwired to seek approval. Children by the age of two will run and comfort another child who is hurt; they want to give and offer love and seek the approval of their parents and other children. Giving and receiving appreciation is what you thrive on.

So feel this positive emotion; give out compliments profusely. Look into the eyes of the one you are appreciating and savor the wondrous warmth. Praise with ardor and enthusiasm somebody's efforts, whether they meet failure or success. Be the first one to applaud, and you will give and receive love like a magnet.

"To forgive is to set a prisoner free and discover that the prisoner was you."

—Lewis B. Smedes

"The weak can never forgive. Forgiveness is the attribute of the strong."

—Mahatma Gandhi

"When a deep injury is done us, we never recover until we forgive."

—Alan Paton

"Forgiveness does not change the past, but it does enlarge the future."

—Paul Boese

"By far the strongest poison to the human spirit is the inability to forgive oneself or another person. Forgiveness is no longer an option but a necessity for healing."

—Caroline Myss

"Holding on to anger, resentment, and hurt only gives you tense muscles, a headache, and a sore jaw from clenching your teeth. Forgiveness gives you back the laughter and the lightness in your life."

—Joan Lunden

FORGIVENESS

The corollary to appreciation is forgiveness. The feelings of anger, jealousy, and hatred are a slow-acting poison that kills the one exercising the emotions, not the one toward whom these ill feelings are directed. Letting go of this baggage releases you from the negativity of fear. For what is forgiveness if not for giving? Forgiveness is a higher act of giving because you conquer your own ego when you give it. And giving, as you know, is the savior of your soul.

Forgiveness works by reducing the stress of the state of being unforgiving—a state of bitterness, anger, hostility, hatred, and fear. All of these emotions have a high physiological price: high blood pressure, cardiovascular disease, lowered immunity, and neurological dysfunction. Those who forgive hold on better to social relationships with family and friends—an essential survival tool in today's lonely times.

You are instantly healed when you forgive because you no longer harbor the toxins of gripes and grudges. You have successfully stifled the little monster inside you.

When a crime or injustice is inflicted on you, you can react by blaming, punishing, hating, and perpetrating the injustice or you can forgive and release yourself and the inflictor from this negative energy.

"Laughter is an instant vacation."
—Milton Berle

"A man isn't poor if he can still laugh."
—Raymond Hitchcock

"Laughter is higher than all pain."
—Elbert Hubbard

"What soap is to the body, laughter is to the soul."
—Yiddish Proverb

"Time spent laughing is time spent with the Gods."
—Japanese Proverb

"We don't laugh because we're happy— we're happy because we laugh."
—William James, psychologist.

LAUGHTER AND HUMOR

Laughter and humor are powerful weapons to weather disappointment and despair. Laughter repairs your soul, rescues you from impossible situations, and re-energizes you. When you laugh with strangers, they become your friends. Laughter overpowers and overtakes your soul so that you forget your troubles and you chase away the ghosts of negativity and delusion. Your self-doubt, illusion, distortion, and confusion are replaced with God's bountiful gift of celebration. This is laughter, and the more you laugh, the better you share the warmth of your heart with others. Laughter may not solve all your problems, but it will certainly dissolve them.

Medically, laughter is indeed the best medicine to relieve stress, reduce pain, aid digestion, improve sleep, lower blood pressure, increase lung capacity, improve circulation, treat depression, and help cure a long list of other ailments.

Laughter is perhaps the most instantly effective therapy to contend with almost any disappointment or despair. When you laugh, you lose all sense of hierarchy vis-à-vis those you laugh with, and your soul is released from the enslavement of your ego.

Laughter is a powerful light switch. Turn it on to instantly replace the darkness of anger and self-doubt with the light of love and joy. No other tool works so quickly and effectively to turn negative energy into positive energy.

"Pessimism leads to weakness, optimism to power."
—William James

"When the aerials are down, and your spirit is covered with snows of cynicism and the ice of pessimism, then you are grown old, even at twenty, but as long as your aerials are up, to catch the waves of optimism, there is hope you may die young at eighty."

—Samuel Ullman

"Many an optimist has become rich by buying out a pessimist."

—Robert G. Allen

"Optimism is joyful searching; pessimism is a prison of fear and a clutching at illusionary safety."
—Kathleen A. Brehony

"Success is going from failure to failure without a loss of enthusiasm."

—Winston Churchill

HOPE AND OPTIMISM

Keep the fountains of hope and optimism alive. Hold your faith fast and firm in God, whatever you perceive Him to be. Often, there will be dark periods in life when nothing seems to be working out. When your fuel gauge is empty and exhausted, hope and optimism will act as the reserve fuel to power you forward.

You are a child of God and have a right to be here. Most of the Jewish survivors of Nazi death camps were the ones who remained stubbornly optimistic. Their bodies were starved and emaciated, but the warmth of their hopes kept them alive. People with a negative attitude think and project only negative tidings, which overpower even a positive-thinking person into becoming a victim of their presence. Vice versa, a positive person is water to the aridity of life's struggles.

Studies have shown that optimistic people fall ill less often than the pessimists, and if they do fall ill, then they recover faster.

In the sequence of thought, word, and deed, thought is the most potent and powerful force, for it is the precursor of the other two. A victory is first won in the mind and then enacted in real life. You need the good, fertile seeds of optimism to flower into success. Big success comes to those who dream big.

Compassion is not simply for others. Be equally compassionate with yourself and so tread softly on your own hopes.

"Courage is fear that has said its prayers."

—Dorothy Bernard

"Prayer draws us near to our own souls."

—Herman Melville

"Prayer is not an old woman's idle amusement. Properly understood and applied, it is the most potent instrument of action."

—Mahatma Gandhi

"When I pray, coincidences happen, and when I don't pray, they don't."

—William Temple

"Prayer may not change things for you, but it for sure changes you for things."

—Samuel M. Shoemaker

"Prayer is exhaling the spirit of man and inhaling the spirit of God."

—Edwin Keith

PRAYER

The healing power of prayer has been studied by several researchers who have amassed amazing results: a healthier immune system, lowered hypertension, and enhanced longevity. Prayer works not only to your own advantage but can also be transmitted as healing energy to others.

Prayer is often understood as an invocation to God or an external force. This gives unsure results because your prayers to win the lottery may go unanswered. The prayers that really work are more of a command to your own internal army of billions and trillions of neurons and cells to join together in courage to overpower the elements. Don't wish it was easier; wish you were better. Don't wish for fewer problems; wish for more skills. Pray for courage and stamina.

Prayer instantly pours courage onto your spirit. It chases away fear and clears the path for you to rise to your best. Prayer is what prods and focuses your energy reserves to rise when you most need them. It is a purifying act that distills your sincerity and honesty.

Prayer is often used as a spare wheel for when there's a flat tire or crisis. But the correct way to use prayer is more like a steering wheel to navigate your destiny, to reach your destination.

To be honest, I've come across some of these tips before. But the way you've put it, I can understand the reasoning behind these specific actions better now. Some of these overlap each other. Even then, it's a good checklist to start from.

And so it is. No rocket science here, just the wisdom of the ages. Most of these behavioral traits have their origins in compassion. They all work to produce the same warm glow effect in you that you've described before. Practice these as feelings, not just intellectual thoughts.

Are there some simple tips to turn on these feelings?

For starters, just once a day make it a point to express gratitude, to appreciate, to forgive, to laugh, and finally to hold your chin up. If things go wrong, summon your internal army through prayer. Linger on any one of these to-dos, or more. Go with your favorite. One way or another, the moment you use these trusted little tools, you'll learn to swim in the energy pool you've chosen.

When you exude goodness toward the people you interact with, you'll end up feeling good and finding the good within you!

You'll feel the change within yourself as you use these pearls to unearth your soul. Make a conscious effort to do this. If you need reminding, stick a copy of the words below onto the back of your cell phone, the inside of your wallet, into a little tag on your key ring, onto the fridge door, your bathroom mirror, or anywhere convenient. Use it as a charm.

- **Feel some Gratitude**
- **Express Appreciation**
- **Give & Forgive Freely**
- **Smile & Laugh Now**
- **Be Positive & Hopeful**
- **Pray with a Pure Heart**

Try out one or more of these actions. That's easy to do. Almost by stealth, your heart pumps up with positive feelings. You can choose to willfully stay in this camp of good feelings for as long as you wish.

You mean you can actually choose the character of your feelings this way?

Abracadabra! Before you know it, you've transposed good feelings over bad ones. You've waded over from the negative energy pool to the positive energy pool. From being controlled by your feelings, you're suddenly in control of your feelings.

Surely there's a catch somewhere. I mean, you can't wave this magic wand over real, life-size situations. Your suggestions will surely work to change a mood, but you can't turn the other cheek—Jesus style—if somebody's just slapped you.

Nobody goes around slapping anybody these days. But even if they did, I suggest that you douse the flames of revenge by instantly focusing on good thoughts within you.

That's not easy! Somebody could cheat you and rob you. Or do a hit and run. Or deceive you. Cause injury and harm.

This is when you need your charm most. Like a rosary. Remember, bad things do happen to good people. You can choose to walk away from the bitterness or drown in it. You can use the charm to clamber over the most challenging problems in life. Remember, you can choose any one feeling to focus on as listed, or more as you wish.

Sometimes the loss is irreparable. If you spend too much time moping about the why of it, you'll merely magnify the problem and suffer tenfold. The point is not why, because there is no answer. The issue at hand is what now. The happiest people are those who are resilient, who bounce back from their woes.

Does the charm work to handle day-to-day stress?

> *"Pain is inevitable, suffering is optional."*
>
> —M. Kathleen Casey

Sure. It's easy to handle physical and mental stress when you've overtaxed your capabilities. The killer stress is emotional, which attacks at least 80 percent of the time. This stress is dangerous; you can't vent it, so you suppress it, and it's like a pressure cooker inside you, causing deep damage to your body and spirit. It's what makes you ill. The charm can certainly help relieve and relax this stress.

Something inside me tells me you could be right.

My pointers won't take away what's bugging you, but it will draw you away from the damaging influence. It will help you cope and then wade out of this pool of negativity. It won't solve your problems, but it'll dissolve your problems.

Doesn't alcohol work the same way?

Ha-ha! That's funny! Compassion puts you in the right energy field to handle your problems in a calm and composed manner. Alcohol merely dulls your senses without resolving anything.

It's worth a try. Does the charm help you handle grief too?

The grief of grievances is easy to overcome using the charm. The grief of bereavement is an emotional journey of reconciliation. The charm is not an instant-acting aspirin, but it will help you handle your grief with the least amount of suffering. It will help you come to terms with your situation and fill your troubled heart with hope and optimism.

I suppose you're right. So that's how it works! In a way, you're tricking your heart to train itself on good feelings—the same feelings of giving and communion that we talked about before.

Yes, indeed. What I've done is to pick out the right actions that provoke positive feelings. The feelings that point you back into a state of positivity.

As a background to getting in touch with yourself, I think that your advice is invaluable. I'm amazed at the simplicity of your prescription.

This is not a cough mixture to swallow down into your tummy—quite the reverse. These are little nuggets encapsulated to help certain feelings to rise up from your tummy, up toward your heart.

So these are the actual positive steps to put you in the right aura of energy.

Precisely! The secret is to starve your own negative energy and stay away from that of others. The negative energy pool is tainted, acidic water that burns you and ages you. Whenever you find yourself in this acid pool, you must quickly wade over to the pure, refreshing and healing waters of the positive energy pool.

You need willpower to wade over.

You need a will, yes. As for the power, this is what I've just given you. Powerful tools to change your destiny at will. These are the means and methods to change your energy field. If there is a panacea to cure all your woes, then this is it—some sort of elixir that will keep you in control of your life. My dear chap, the power to alter your destiny is now yours.

The tips you've given—they work to rivet you on a feeling of compassion, of positivity. That's the underlying theme.

And so it is! When you're down in the dumps, defeated and deflated, try these steps. The only way to mask the negative impact of bad things is by superimposing positive thoughts on top of the negativity. When things go wrong, avoid the automatic responses of anger and blame. Instead, try to focus on positive things. This will help you focus on solutions, rather than problems.

Overwrite, overlap, override, overcome. Isn't it paradoxical that the right way to discipline your inner monster is to offer him sympathy?

That's the key to taming the monster inside you—the anti-God. Now you have the code to my DNA. You can actually convert yourself into a powerfully positive person and create the world of your liking. Free yourself from the swamps of negativity and fly high, higher, and ever higher. Liberated from the poison of negativity, you'll become more in control of your life. You will constantly stay in an elevated mood and will learn to create your destiny. This is your self-actualization, to discover yourself as a part of God and experience Him firsthand.

You've used some powerful words to describe the euphoria of positive energy. Is there a surefire way to actually *feel* this happening? To test out both the short-term and long-term effects of your prescription?

Do you still need to be convinced? What's your gut feeling about all that I've said?

THE END IS NIGH

- Your thoughts, feelings, and attitude to the world are joyful and optimistic, not based on fear and pessimism.

- You don't dwell on past disappointments that provoked fear.

- You don't mull so much on what others are thinking of you, or suspect what they are up to. Instead, you're more focused on your own feelings.

- You prefer to walk away from anger and conflict, rather than hang around even as a bystander.

- You worry less about what will happen to you tomorrow.

- You are more satisfied with yourself and your lot in life.

- You find it easier to relate to others. You feel more connected to everybody and to nature.

- Your urge to control others is dampened. You are comfortable with letting them be to go as they please.

- You are not quick to place blame on somebody or something when things go wrong. Instead you accept chance mishaps as passing clouds.

- Your urge to "teach a lesson" to annoying, erring people is gone.

- You live in, and connect to, the present moment and take greater pleasure in day-to-day activities.

- You radiate love. You feel charged and alive all the time, a conduit to both receive and give love.

- You derive a deep inner satisfaction in being of use to others and the world.

My gut feeling is positive, excited, and in great admiration of your advice. I just wanted to know about the clues to look out for—to make sure it's working.

Okay, Mr. Neat List. I'll set down some of the major changes in your personality that you'll notice. In stages you'll actually feel them all, one by one.

Wow! I've felt some of these feelings myself, and you've now put them into words. It's amazing! This sounds simple, but it's how you measure your inner peace.

You have a penchant for detail!

I feel a great calm even as I'm stunned by the simplicity of what you've just said. I feel a breathless excitement. I think I can take on the world.

The inside world. When you've conquered your inside world, you'll discover a new, boundless energy to conquer the outside one. Your vision will become clear only when you look into your heart. As Carl Jung said, "Who looks outside, dreams. Who looks inside, awakens."

This seems such a natural and simple way to change your life force, from a radiation that saps your strength to one that nourishes it.

That's a good description. You can choose to step out of the field of fear, fantasy, obsession, anxiety, and emotional debris. Greed, anger, and hatred bring restlessness, aggression, and depression.

Now you have the power to turn your back on this dark dungeon and enter the force field of protection that your compassion will provide for you. The goodness of your soul will strengthen your spirit.

I can't wait to try out the charm!

Don't look for instant results, but those from patience. The prospect of the results is assured, but they're perceived in retrospect. Use the charm in everyday life, routinely, on your way to work, during any quiet moment you get. Use it especially when your inner monster provokes you. Use it to avert and sideline a bout of anger and depression. The more provoked you are, the more determined you should become to stick with your positive energy and stay inside its soothing aura. Wait out the temptation to hit back. Breathe in, breathe out.

Wait a half hour, wait an hour. Now look back. Look how you safely doused the flames of negativity. Feel relieved and relaxed.

I can use this charm anywhere, anytime.

If your attention lapses, refocus. There is no right way and wrong way to dwell and mull on these pointers. The way that works for you is the best way. With the answer in your hands, you'll soon be taken over by waves of soothing, refreshing positive energy—the life force that nurtures and nourishes you.

I'm going to use this charm every chance I get!

Like a newfound toy? Even if that is so, this is one toy that's ageless, timeless.

I wish you good luck.

CHAPTER 10

THE LAST LAUGH

 I feel a strange aura that surrounds me when I'm in the compassionate mode. It's like a funny welling up of the heart all the way to my throat. It seems impossible to be angry or feel any sort of ill will toward anybody. Like a great calm has descended over me, blanketing me in love.

You're reading from the checklist I gave you!

 I'm just so breathlessly excited with this fantastic formula you've given. I'm just airing my feelings as they descend on me.

Take your time to toy with the techniques you now have.

In the meantime, I must say that you've raised the dust on many questions that have haunted the human race for thousands of years.

And you wiped the dust off the answers. Now they're visible.

I found a patient listener in you. Not bigoted and befooled by big talk, but open to the truth. I enjoyed our conversation.

 That's a big compliment, coming from you. I value the time you gave me. You're not really so anti-Godly, after all. The way I see it, you're God yourself!

I am a creation of God and therefore a part of God, just as you are.

I'm human, but you're superhuman.

Maybe that's so. I'm God's trusted lieutenant to soak up your hatred, your blame, and misgivings, to fill you up with sorrow in order to soften your heart and make it humane. To make sure that bad things happen to all of you so that you can come up with your best. I am as important to creation as God is. I'm here to point you to the glory of God.

If you are a part of God, then you've reached the pinnacle of salvation as a soul. Your experiential journey of "been there, done that" is over and you now sit on God's lap. Fully conscious of the connection you have with the Almighty.

And yet my work in this world is thankless. I am despised and detested. I sometimes wish for a refuge from the recriminations I'm subjected to, but that's another story. Well, now there's at least one of you who understands me for who and what I am!

I'm privileged to stand before you in the here and now—talking with you, walking with you—even though you're supposed to be evil.

Evil is the other side of the same coin as righteousness. The two are conjoined at birth and perforce must learn to live together through adulthood into a ripe old age. Just as each ego has an alter ego, so must you come to terms with your unbelieving, paranoid, skeptic self.

That's a tall order.

And a good challenge for the tall in spirit, the tall in stride!

And so, am I to pray for a good height? To become tall enough to jump over these hurdles?

Well said. Your salvation is to reach the height where you can look from up above at all the tiny teasers and twisters of life. And for this, I wish you fair tidings!

Before we say good-bye, let me congratulate you in return. I've developed a fair amount of respect for you too.

I'm not a patch on you, nothing lofty. I'm just a stumped simpleton.

Don't underrate yourself. You may not know it, but everything, repeat everything, in life happens for a reason.

Amidst the clamor, a passing remark from somebody, or a chance meeting, the newspaper unwittingly open at just the right page, or an accidental exposure to some idea, a clue here, a concept there: These may be chance events, but in effect it is God's unseen hand pointing you to your potential, your destiny.

I don't get it. What do you mean?

Go back to yourself ten years ago. No, fifteen or even twenty years ago. At that time—as you rightly say—you were absorbed in your career, in making money, in an idyllic social setting.

And my soul was lost.

Not lost, but asleep.

Until it was stolen, by laughteryoga. A chance event changed my life!

What a laugh! Do you really think it was by chance? Do you think people pick up cues and signals to take their interest forward by chance? Do you think Edison invented the light bulb because a flash of some heavenly inspiration struck him?

I can't say.

My dear chap, long before your so-called spark ignites you, you spend years and years rendering yourselves ready, or open, to receive certain signals from the universe. When your conscience incites you to move forward, then you're accessible to the little nods and nudges that the elements scatter under your nose.

What do you mean? Is it that we are for years emotionally predisposed toward a certain action before we actually proceed to act?

Absolutely. If one day you decide to become a vegetarian, then you've been toying with this as a concern, as a sensitivity, long before Decision Day. Likewise, if somebody volunteers for the Red Cross today, it's because that's been his or her calling for years. In elementary terms, the world picks up the scent of your leanings long before you do. It predisposes you, prepares you, and then pushes you toward the fruition of your calling.

Your intentions have spent a long time below the ground before germinating and sprouting. Along the way, little emotive, intuitive taps and jabs from day-to-day events kick off the flowering process.

Your soul is unconsciously or subconsciously looking for the inklings and innuendos suggested by your surroundings—ideas that will feed and fertilize the seed of longing within you.

Instinctively, I admire your reasoning because I can feel this truth in my bones.

And this brings me to you. If one day you decide to write a book, then in fact you'll have been collecting little nuggets to put into the book for a long, long time before you recognize the intention. And it may be years and years later that your book actually sees the light of day.

You're psychic! You read me like an open book!

A few minutes ago I said that "…when your soul is riveted on meaningful intentions, then God sheds his veil and rearranges, recreates your world of possibilities. God pumps you up with courage and clears your hurdles…"

When the conditions are right and God is impressed with the purity of your intentions, He actually tweaks the environment to tilt it toward you.

You're joking! You mean my dreams will come true?

And with my blessings. But before that, don't belittle yourself before your own eyes. You're wrong to say that "It was purely by chance that I bumped into this laughter activity that changed my life." Wrong because years, decades before you actually found your purpose, you were priming and preparing yourself for it. Making yourself ready to receive it.

Your stimulus did not come in a flash from heaven, but from within yourself. It is because your inner being, your soul, was captivated by an urge to seek meaning that you rose forward. All the hints and cues and signs that were hidden suddenly leapt to life. Because you were compassionate to the world and your role in it.

You mean I was in a frame of mind ready to receive the laughter activity.

Exactly. It didn't happen as some chance event. It was meant to happen. God saw your years and decades of preparation for it and then put the two of you together.

I'm touched by your kind words. But often people think that I'm a clown. Is this true?

You are by blood a king, by soul a saint, in heart a clown.

I'm speechless. Dumbfounded.

They say there's nothing funnier than a sad-faced clown. To me, there's nothing sadder than a funny-faced one. A joker best understands and feels the pain of others and makes it his calling to disperse and dispel their distress. Is that not compassion?

A clown has a tough act to follow. He cannot afford the luxury of shedding his own tears because he's taken up the job of wiping the rivers of tears around him. His submerges his sorrows in recognizing the world's sorrows and makes that his calling.

> *"No one is more profoundly sad as one who laughs too much."*
>
> —Jean Paul Sartre

I could cry right now, but they say that real men don't cry.

Only the real men cry, and those who can't are unreal. Isn't that what you tell your laughter groups?

I show them how to revive and renew themselves. I feel I have a responsibility to those I teach to laugh, and to the hundreds and thousands I still have to meet for this purpose.

> *"Those who do not know how to weep with their whole heart don't know how to laugh either."*
>
> —Golda Meir

And that makes you a healer. Jest is your joy!

That's a laugh! Many people laugh *at* me, many *for* me, and many more *with* me.

As long as they laugh because of you, you'll do fine. And I say this not just in jest.

You're right. I can laugh because I make others laugh. It's the only way I know to enjoy **The Last Laugh.**

"In this life he laughs longest who laughs last."

—John Masefield

POSTWORD

August 2008

In the spirit of laughter, at Vishwa's request I am overjoyed to write this postword instead of the standard foreword. Vishwa's account of his laughter experiences makes delightful reading. This is an eloquent narrative of the inner spirit of laughter and the magic spell it casts over both the leader and participants of a laughteryoga session.

Since I pioneered the concept in 1995, the laughteryoga movement now spans over ten thousand laughter clubs in forty-five countries. I am pleased to borrow Vishwa's words to describe this as a journey of the soul—a journey in which I have found few so passionate, dedicated, and gifted as Vishwa.

Vishwa has the unstinting heart of a true philanthropist and donates large slices of his resources to charitable causes. In Vishwa's unique style, this book is a gift to the world, meant to touch and enrich its readers with the true meaning of life. Many of Vishwa's views are unorthodox, but they remain fresh and interesting.

Vishwa is an adept master at expressing his feelings, which seem to float off the pages of this book to enter the mind and soul of the reader.

I am proud to have been the stimulus that helped Vishwa to flower the way he has. He has now become a maestro in his own right and a close friend and partner in the world laughteryoga movement.

This book is a treasure trove of the wonderful feelings that alight on those who seek to get in touch with their inner selves. In Vishwa you have a guru of gurus, who knows how to lead you into a world of meaningful love and laughter. I am privileged to recommend this book to everyday people as a living inspiration, and to laughteryoga participants as compulsory reading.

MADAN KATARIA
Founder and President
Laughter International

PONDERABLE POINTS
References and Further Reading

Money and Happiness

Hedonism (the maximization of pleasurable activity) in its initial and infrequent stages leads to higher levels of happiness, but tapers off quickly, while hedonism in larger doses is actually related to lower levels of happiness.
—**Ruut Veenhoven, Erasmus University, Rotterdam, Netherlands.**

Studies show that the happiest people are those who help others and donate to worthy causes. This is endorsed by a study at Columbia University which concludes that doing good deeds causes a rise in dopamine and other brain chemicals known to boost mood. Our motives for giving really don't matter, but the more you give, the more happiness you get.
—**Dan Baker, *What Happy People Know*, and Michael Liebowitz, MD, Columbia University**

An ambitious analysis of over 150 studies on wealth and happiness shows that there is no correlation between rising economic output and personal satisfaction. The analysis concluded that happiness is not derived from prosperity but from relationships, productivity, fulfillment, and community involvement.
—**Sharon Begley, *The Wall Street Journal, Science Journal***

The saying that "money can't buy happiness" was confirmed by a survey that polled 1471 Australians, revealing that 91 percent of those surveyed rated factors other than money as bringing a smile to their lips, while money made only 6 percent of the people smile. These findings support the theory that people derive more happiness from relationships than money.

—A.C Nielsen Survey, Australia

Researchers in Sweden concluded that working hard and using one's skills to reach a goal brings more self-satisfaction than the goal itself. Money, a holiday, and even success bring only temporary joy because of the "habituation effect," which occurs within a few weeks.

—Bengt Bruelde, Gothenburg University, Sweden

SOCIETY AND HAPPINESS

A survey of 6,000 persons in Switzerland concluded that happiness is directly related to political freedom. The more developed the institutions of direct democracy, the happier individuals are, pointing to a view that people are happier when participating in what affects them.

—Bruno S. Frey and Alois Stutzer, "Happiness Prospers in Democracy," *Journal of Happiness Studies,* **March 2000.**

Happiness is infectious, concludes a research of 4,700 people in Framingham as part of a heart study from 1983 to 2003. The study found that happy people passed on their cheer to people unknown to them, and that this transferred happiness lasted for up to a year. The researchers contend that each happy friend boosts your own happiness chances by 9 percent and having grumpy friends decreases it by about 7 percent. If a happy friend lives within a mile of you, it increases the likelihood of your being happy by 25 percent.

—*The British Medical Journal,* reporting on a study led by Professor Nicholas Christakis from Harvard Medical School.

Dan Baker and Cameron Stauth, in *What Happy People Know,* outline that all our fears of loss, rejection, death, and failure can be grouped into three basic fears (1) Survival (2) Fear of Not Having Enough and (3) Fear of Not Being Enough, and so long as fear pervades our emotions, our pursuit of happiness will be destructive for ourselves and others.
—Dan Baker and Cameron Stauth, Rodale 2003.

MOOD REGULATION AND HAPPINESS

A large component of happiness maintenance involves mood regulation. According to a study by Gross and John, thought suppression actually intensifies and prolongs unhappiness. Research also shows, however, that focusing on the causes and consequences of a negative mood is counter-productive because it serves to maintain and intensify the negative effects of such moods. This indicates that one should neither suppress nor dwell on unhappiness but simply let it be.
—Thayer et al., 1994; Gross and John, 2003; Lyubomirsky and Tkach, 2004

People who optimistically pursued their objectives are more likely to achieve their goals, whereas those who expect failure are more likely to give up. Happy people are able to sustain their happiness because after experiencing failure, they do not dwell on negative self-reflection.
—Allison Abbe, Chris Tkach and Sonja Lyubomirsky, "The Art of Living by Dispositionally Happy People," *Journal of Happiness Studies,* **December 2003.**

Research shows that "smiling" or "acting happy" as expressive behavior can lift negative moods. Direct attempts at happiness are significantly related to experienced happiness, and it is thought that the expression of emotion heightens the intensity of the emotional experience.
—Morris and Reilly (1987)

Recent experiments studied participants assigned to physically express happiness, anger, fear, or sadness show that simply acting out the behaviors associated with particular emotions serves to bring upon or intensify that particular emotion. The upshot is that by acting happy, it may be possible to make oneself happy.

—Duclos et al., 1989; Strack et al., 1988

Increasingly, modern psychotherapy lets bygones be bygones. Until recently, the belief was that digging up the past would provide answers to heal the problems at hand. Current research, however, has convinced many therapists that reviewing the past is not only unnecessary, but could be counterproductive. This modern approach to cognitive behavioral therapy of focusing on *today* rather than *yesterday* is more effective, as studied over the last twenty years.

—John C. Norcross, Professor of Psychology, University of Scranton

Older people with positive perceptions of aging lived 7.5 years longer than those with less positive ideas, and were happier.

—Herzog and Rodgers, 1981, based on research performed at Yale University

HEALTH AND HAPPINESS

Research conducted on forty-nine end-stage kidney failure patients as compared with healthy people concluded that the levels of happiness were about the same for the two groups, lending credence to the contention that happiness is a matter of choice as an internal "set point." The study also found that the healthy people greatly overestimated how unhappy the sick ones would be, and the sick people overestimated how happy healthy ones would be.

—Eric Nagourney, *NY Times,* **February 15, 2005, reporting on research conducted by Dr. Jason Riis and covered by the** *Journal of Experimental Psychology.*

Which day of the week has the most frequent attacks? Mondays, of course, because of the stress of returning to work and the pressure of facing up to demanding situations. A number of studies of various populations over several years concluded that the lowest number of heart attack deaths occur on weekends, jump significantly on Mondays and drop again on Tuesdays.

—*The European Journal of Epidemiology,* **as reported in the** *New York Times*

Positive feelings about oneself and being happy indeed are directly correlated with an increase in a person's length of life. Happy people tend to have better functioning immune systems and lower levels of the stress hormone **cortisol**. They are also more likely to recover from major surgery. When a person has a happy experience, the body chemistry improves and blood pressure/heart rate both tend to fall.

—**Diener et al. (2001), Ryff and Singer (2003), Goleman (1996), and Rosenkranz et al. (2003), and Davidson et al. (2000)**

Being grateful boosts the immune system and is good for health. Grateful people are generally more optimistic, happier , suffer less depression, and are more resilient in the face of stress.

—**Robert A. Emmons, University of California,** *Journal of Positive Psychology*

Spirituality and Happiness

A study trying to find a relationship between religious beliefs and happiness concluded that happiness is not associated with people's material accumulation but with their perceived inner world. Happy people see their religion not so much as something they "do" as what they "are."

—**William R. Swinyard, Ah-Keung-Kau, and Hui-Yin Phua, "Happiness, Materialism, and Religious Experience in the U.S. and Singapore,"** *Journal of Happiness Studies,* **March 2001.**

Buddhists who seem serene really are according to neuroscientists who have used sophisticated scanning techniques which show that the areas of the brain linked to positive emotions and good mood light up constantly in Buddhists. The study concluded that mindfulness and meditation caused Buddhists to be less shocked and flustered and experience a continuously higher level of joy.

—Professor Owen Flanagan of Duke University, *New Scientist Magazine*

A recent study at Cha Hospital in Seoul, South Korea showed that when strangers prayed for some of the women in an *in vitro* fertilization clinic, the pregnancy rate of those prayed for doubled.

Dr. Elizabeth Fischer Targ of the Pacific College of Medicine in San Francisco tested the effects of prayer on critically ill AIDS patients and found that those prayed for were much stronger and had fewer hospital stays than those not receiving any remote prayers.

The National Institute of Healthcare Research (NIHR) has reviewed nearly thirty studies on the influence of spirituality on health and concluded that religious people live longer than those less spiritual across the board.

—Rise Birnbaum, *Arrive Magazine*

If you enjoyed reading this book, please send us your comments at
feedback@whostolemysoul.com

You may also order the full page inspirational pictures with words in this book as laminated frameables or posters. Full details are available on
www.whostolemysoul.com